Bertolt Brecht: Plays, Poetry, Prose

Edited by JOHN WILLETT *and* RALPH MANHEIM

The Collected Plays

Volume One Part Three

16

Brecht's Plays, Poetry and Prose
annotated and edited in hardback and paperback
by John Willett and Ralph Manheim

Collected Plays

Vol. 1 (*hardback only*)	Baal; Drums in the Night; In the Jungle of Cities; The Life of Edward II of England; A Respectable Wedding; The Beggar; Driving Out a Devil; Lux in Tenebris; The Catch
Vol. 1i	Baal (*paperback only*)
Vol. 1ii	A Respectable Wedding and other one-act plays (*paperback only*)
Vol. 1iii	Drums in the Night (*paperback only*)
Vol. 1iv	In the Jungle of Cities (*paperback only*)
Vol. 2i	Man equals Man; The Elephant Calf
Vol. 2ii	The Threepenny Opera
Vol. 2iii	The Rise and Fall of the City of Mahagonny; The Seven Deadly Sins
*Vol. 3i	Saint Joan of the Stockyards
*Vol. 3ii	The Baden-Baden Cantata; The Flight over the Ocean; He Who Said Yes; He Who Said No; The Decision
*Vol. 4i	The Mother; The Exception and the Rule; The Horatii and the Curiatii
*Vol. 4ii	Round Heads and Pointed Heads
*Vol. 4iii	Señora Carrar's Rifles; Fear and Misery of the Third Reich
Vol. 5i	Life of Galileo
Vol. 5ii	Mother Courage and her Children
*Vol. 5iii	The Trial of Lucullus; Dansen; What's the Price of Iron?
*Vol. 6i	The Good Person of Szechwan
*Vol. 6ii	The Resistible Rise of Arturo Ui
*Vol. 6iii	Mr Puntila and his Man Matti
Vol. 7	The Visions of Simone Machard; Schweyk in the Second World War; The Caucasian Chalk Circle; The Duchess of Malfi
*Vol. 8i	The Days of the Commune
*Vol. 8ii	Turandot; Report from Herrnburg
*Vol. 8iii	Downfall of the Egoist Johann Fatzer; The Life of Confucius; The Breadshop; The Salzburg Dance of Death

Poetry
Poems 1913–1956

Prose
Brecht on Theatre
Diaries 1920–1922
*Short Stories 1921–1946
*Selected Essays

* in preparation

The following plays are also available (in paperback only) in unannotated editions:

The Caucasian Chalk Circle; The Days of the Commune; The Good Person of Szechwan; The Life of Galileo; The Measures Taken and other Lehrstücke; The Messingkauf Dialogues; Mr Puntila and his Man Matti; The Mother; The Resistible Rise of Arturo Ui; Saint Joan of the Stockyards

Bertolt Brecht Collected Plays

Volume One Part Three

Edited by
John Willett
and Ralph Manheim

Drums in the Night
Translated by John Willett

Eyre Methuen · London

This paperback edition first published in Great Britain in 1980
by Eyre Methuen Ltd, 11 New Fetter Lane, London EC4P 4EE,
by arrangement with Suhrkamp Verlag, Frankfurt am Main

Previously published in hardback in Brecht's Collected Plays
Volume 1 1918–1923 by Methuen & Co Ltd in 1970

ISBN 0 413 47470 4

Reproduced, printed and bound in Great Britain by
Fakenham Press Limited, Fakenham, Norfolk

Introduction

Drums in the Night is the second of four full-length plays (the others being *Baal, In the Jungle of Cities* and *The Life of Edward II of England*) which Brecht wrote in Bavaria before moving to Berlin in the autumn of 1924. In spring 1918, when he began work on the first of them, he was just twenty and a new student at Munich university. Six and a half years later he was a recognized, if controversial writer and the winner of a major literary prize. The best directors and actors of the day were performing his plays; he had also written many poems and short stories and directed one remarkable production. He had just been on the staff of the Munich Kammerspiele, one of the most enterprising small theatres in Germany, where his first and so far most successful play had been performed. Now he was about to go as a 'dramaturg', or literary adviser, to Max Reinhardt's Deutsches Theater in Berlin, at that time one of the world's three or four leading theatres.

Born on 10 February 1898, Brecht had been brought up in Augsburg, about forty miles west of Munich. His father, a native of the Black Forest, was sales director of the Haindl paper works there; his mother died in May 1920. *Baal*, whose first version was finished by July 1918, reflects much of the imaginary world of himself and his group of Augsburg friends, as well as the taverns and physical surroundings of the old city. For a few months just before and after the armistice of November 1918 he served as a medical orderly in a local army hospital, but had returned to Munich by February 1919, the early days of the Bavarian Soviet, during which he dashed off the first version of *Drums in the Night*. There he showed both plays to Lion Feuchtwanger, the author of *Jew Süss*, who was then living in Munich and had recently met him for the first time. His own drama professor Artur Kutscher was always bitterly critical of his work, but Feuchtwanger was encouraging, so that he began to make contact with publishers and, at the end of the summer vacation, to write theatre criticisms for the Augsburg Socialist paper. Five one-act plays, *A Respectable Wedding, The Beggar, Driving out a Devil, Lux in Tenebris* and *The Catch*, are also thought to have been mainly written that year, as well as a wealth of lost or unfinished works.

Baal was accepted by Feuchtwanger's own publisher Georg Müller, who had also published Wedekind's collected plays, but was withdrawn when already in proof for fear of the censorship. *Drums in the Night* was shown by Feuchtwanger to the Kammerspiele 'dramaturg' Rudolf Frank, who at some point in the summer of 1920 accepted it for production. Neither publication nor production in fact materialized for another two years, but the encouragement to Brecht was obvious. He left the university in the summer of 1921 and in November set out to try his luck in Berlin, a much more important city from the theatrical point of view.

The expedition was less successful than he had hoped. Neither the Deutsches Theater nor the State Theatre under Leopold Jessner would make any promises, and although Brecht was asked to direct Arnolt Bronnen's play *Vatermord* for the experimental Junge Bühne, it ended disastrously with a walk-out of the actors. He himself was taken to hospital suffering from undernourishment, due no doubt in part to the galloping currency inflation. But at least he made many connections or friendships which were to be important for his work: notably Bronnen (with whom he began collaborating on film treatments and various joint theatrical projects), Herbert Ihering the critic of the *Berliner Börsen-Courier* (a lifelong supporter, whose paper was later to serve as a launching-platform for many of his ideas), and Moritz Seeler the organizer of the Junge Bühne (who was to produce *Life Story of the Man Baal* in 1926). By the time of his return to Augsburg at Easter he had also completed the first version of *In the Jungle*.

In Bavaria 1922 was a Brecht year. Soon after his return the Munich Residenztheater accepted *In the Jungle*, thanks to the recommendations of its artistic adviser Jacob Geis and of its new chief director Erich Engel, who had arrived a few months earlier from his native Hamburg. *Baal* was at last published (by Gustav Kiepenheuer of Potsdam), while 29 September saw the première of *Drums in the Night*. Clearly this was very different from later Brecht productions, for Otto Falckenberg, the head of the Kammerspiele, staged it in expressionist style with angular poses and sets to match by his own staff designer Otto Reigbert. But Ihering came from Berlin to review it, and in the *Berliner Börsen-Courier* of 5 October he wrote that 'At 24 the writer Bert Brecht has changed Germany's literary complexion overnight. Bert Brecht has given our time a new tone, a new melody, a new vision.' Here too was 'a physical sense of chaos and decay':

Hence the unparallelled creative force of his language. It is a language you can feel on your tongue, in your gums, your ear, your spinal column.

Ihering was known to be the judge for that year's award of the Kleist Prize. This had been founded in 1911 by a group of Kleist enthusiasts to celebrate the centenary of the poet's death, and was intended for writers who had yet to establish themselves. Up to its abolition in 1932 it was probably the most significant literary award in Germany, having previously been given to the playwrights Sorge, Unruh, Hasenclever and Jahnn, while in 1923–5 it went to Musil, Barlach and Zuckmayer. On 13 November the *Berliner Börsen-Courier* announced that it had gone to Brecht, and not for *Drums in the Night* only but for all three of his completed plays. 'Brecht's linguistic power,' said Ihering's citation,

> is even more richly developed in *Baal* and *In the Jungle*. His language is vivid without being deliberately poetic, symbolical without being over literary. Brecht is a dramatist because his language is felt physically and in the round.

Because *Drums in the Night* was generally regarded as the prize-winning play it was widely performed all over Germany, notably in Berlin immediately before Christmas, when Falckenberg again directed it for the Deutsches Theater with a first-rate cast. Brecht always claimed that he had only written it to make money, and certainly it differs in several ways from his other works. Alone of those in this volume it seems to contain no anticipations of his later plays.

In Munich for two nights after the première it was followed by a midnight show called *The Red Grape* (*Die rote Zibebe*, a name at one time given to the tavern in Act 4, and also used of the moon which hangs so conspicuously over the action). This was described as an 'improvisation in two scenes by Bert Brecht and Karl Valentin', the latter being a famous Munich music-hall comedian. In the first scene Max Schreck, the actor who played Glubb, was the Freakshow Landlord who opened a series of curtained cabins, each containing a performer who stepped out to do a solo turn. The programme shows that these included the sailor-poet Joachim Ringelnatz, the reciter Ludwig Hardt, Brecht himself singing songs, and the dancer Valeska Gert, though for the second performance Brecht seems to have been replaced by his fellow-poet Klabund. The second scene was a sketch called 'Christmas Evening' by Valentin, whom a short programme note by Brecht compared with

Chaplin, among other things for his 'virtually complete rejection
of mimicry and cheap psychology'. Valentin's influence has sometimes been seen in Brecht's farcical one-acters, though Brecht himself acknowledged it rather as affecting his work as a director,
particularly his use of grouping.

That October Brecht was appointed to the Kammerspiele's
dramaturgical and directing staff, where his main task was the
adaptation and production of Marlowe's *Edward II*. The actual
writing of this play, which is very largely an original work, must
have taken place mainly in the winter of 1922–3, since the Berlin
State Theatre started showing an interest in it early in the new year.
It was done in collaboration with Feuchtwanger, whom Brecht
saw frequently throughout 1923 and who is said to have inspired
the speech characteristics of Shlink in *In the Jungle*. It was not however performed till the next year, and although there were two
more Brecht premières in 1923, neither was at the Kammerspiele
itself. First *In the Jungle* was staged at the Residenztheater on 9 May
by Engel, with settings by Brecht's school-friend Caspar Neher:
the beginning of a lifelong collaboration between the three men.
Jessner of the State Theatre came from Berlin, as did Ihering, who
again wrote enthusiastically, though not without observing that
to anyone insensitive to its language the play must appear a muddle.
This the local critics bore out; the three-hour performance was
poorly received; it ran for only six evenings, and altogether was a
disastrous enough flop to occasion the sacking of the theatre's
artistic adviser. Nor was *Baal* in Leipzig at the end of the year any
more successful. Alvin Kronacher's production at the Old Theatre
on 8 December was taken off by order of the city council within
a week, and the director reprimanded. It brought an interesting
press controversy between Ihering and his rival Alfred Kerr as to
the relative originality of Brecht and Toller, but Kerr was undoubtedly right when he wrote that 'The only hope for a Baalade
like this is as a posthumous fragment . . .'. For the text as we have it
was not performed again for another forty years.

The rehearsals for *Edward II* began that autumn under Brecht's
own direction. Brecht also supplied the music; the sets were again
by Neher, and as in the two previous Munich Brecht productions
the actor Erwin Faber played the lead. The première on 19 March
1924 was somewhat thrown out by the drunkenness of one of the
principal actors, but the local critics appreciated Brecht's success in
conveying his ballad-like conception of the story (he apparently
had the scene titles and dates announced before each episode),

while Ihering was impressed by his handling of the ensemble scenes and the careful dissection of the long speeches. Knowing something of Brecht's as yet unformulated theoretical ideas, he realized that the audience with which he most sympathized was that for boxing matches, sporting events and incidents in the street, and attributed to this novel orientation part of the success of the production. Looking back two years later he saw it as something more: a major turning-point in the German theatre's understanding of the classics. For here had been an attempt at demonumentalization, an appeal for 'not so much plaster . . .' (the title of one of Brecht's subsequent essays), in which

> He did not analyse the characters; he set them at a distance . . .
> He called for a report on the events.

Viewed from 1926 it seemed like an early example of the 'epic' style.

Brecht's Munich period came to an end with the 1923-4 theatrical season, for once established in Berlin he remained based there until he went into exile in 1933. Only the one-acters had not been performed by the time of his move. *Baal, Drums in the Night* and *Edward* were all in print, while the *Hauspostille*, his first book of poems, was enjoying something of an underground reputation, having been announced as early as 1922, five years before its actual publication. That first winter in Berlin he was to have the rare distinction (for a young author) of two productions in the major theatres: *Edward II* directed by Jürgen Fehling (this gifted director's only Brecht production) at the State Theatre, with Werner Krauss as Mortimer and Faber once more as Edward, and *Jungle* at the Deutsches Theater directed by Engel, who had been lured to Berlin by Max Reinhardt a few months before Brecht. The outstanding young actor Fritz Kortner turned down a part in Reinhardt's *St Joan* in order to play Shlink: another indication of the interest already stimulated by Brecht's early work.

II

If the Bavarian years made Brecht's name they also established the main lines of argument for and against his work, with Kerr and Ihering respectively as counsel for the prosecution and the defence. Already the point at issue was his literary borrowings, and a number of later attacks on him were foreshadowed in Kerr's *Baal* critique, with its dismissal of the play as second-hand Büchner and Grabbe.

'The gifted Brecht,' he wrote, 'is a frothing plagiarist.' To which Ihering countered:

> A writer's productivity can be seen in his relationship with old themes. In *Schweiger* Werfel invented a 'hitherto unheard of story' and was none the less imitative in every respect. Brecht was fired by Marlowe's *Edward II* and was creative through and through.

At the same time Brecht had been able to build the nucleus of his subsequent team of supporters and collaborators: first and foremost Neher, then Engel, the rather older Feuchtwanger, Kortner, Homolka, Klabund's actress wife Carola Neher and the playwright Marieluise Fleisser, all of them people who have left their individual marks on the German theatre. Here Brecht's personal magnetism clearly played a part: something to which there have been many tributes, starting with Feuchtwanger's fictional picture of him as the engineer Pröckl in his novel *Success* (1931). The first three plays all bore dedications: to his school-friend George Pfanzelt (the 'Orge' of the poems), to Bie Banholzer who bore his illegitimate son Frank (killed in the war) and to Marianne his first wife, whom he married in 1922. With *Edward II* this practice came to an end.

These were Brecht's pre-collectivist, indeed in a sense his pre-political years. He undoubtedly had opinions, many of them progressive and even revolutionary, but they were far from systematic, and politics and economics were wholly absent from what we know of his reading. On the other hand it was an extraordinarily tense and eventful time for Germany in general and Bavaria in particular, and Brecht was much too sensitive a writer not to reflect this in his work. A good deal has been made of his supposed pacifism in the First World War – though his schoolboy writings show that in fact he set out from a conventionally patriotic attitude and hardly developed beyond concern at the casualties – and of the impact made on him by his military service, which in fact was done on his own doorstep and in a hospital for venereal diseases, and started only a month or two before the end of the war. Several of the *Hauspostille* poems which are held to express his post-war sense of release had in fact already been written by then. Nor is there any evidence that he was more than a spectator of the revolutionary movements of November 1918, when the monarchy fell, and the first months of 1919, when Munich and Augsburg were governed by Soviets following Kurt Eisner's murder and the short-lived Spartacist revolt in Berlin.

Yet the 'Legend of the Dead Soldier' which he wrote in 1918 and took into *Drums in the Night* (see pp. 39 and 57) is always supposed to have earned him a place on the Munich Nazis' black list, while the play itself, though their paper the *Völkischer Beobachter* thought that it 'at any rate showed something of the idiocy of the November Revolution', struck none of the liberal critics as an unfair picture. It was certainly a very confused one, as the muddle over the dating of the action will confirm, and Brecht himself came to judge it in the severest terms, very nearly suppressing the play altogether. The revolutionary setting, however, was only a background to the real drama, and it had an instinctive poetic power which was not to be found in Brecht's later amendments.

The element of revolt in his writing of this time was largely directed against his own middle-class background: the satirical first scene of *Baal*, for instance, and the first two acts of *Drums in the Night*. Much of his reading, too, was exotic-escapist, as can be seen from the allusions in these plays to Gauguin and *Treasure Island* and Rudyard Kipling, and certainly this partly explains Brecht's interest in Rimbaud, whose elevated prose underlies Garga's 'psalmodizing' in *In the Jungle* (cf. Brecht's own semi-prose 'Psalms') and whose relationship with Verlaine was surely the model for that of Baal and Ekart. 'How boring Germany is!' says a note of 18 June 1920. 'It's a good average country, its pale colours and its surfaces are beautiful, but what inhabitants!' 'What's left?' he concluded: 'America!' That year he read two novels about Chicago, J. V. Jensen's *The Wheel* (which has never appeared in English) and Upton Sinclair's *The Jungle*, and when he began work on his own *In the Jungle* it was under their influence, intensified no doubt by his first experience of 'the crushing impact of cities' (about which he wrote an early poem) in the hard winter of 1921–2.

By the time of its first performance the French occupation of the Ruhr had given a great stimulus to nationalism throughout Germany, and not least to the Nazis in Bavaria. The *Völkischer Beobachter* particularly detested this play, claiming that the audience was full of Jews and that the Chinese characters spoke Yiddish. A month later Brecht and Bronnen heard Adolf Hitler addressing a meeting in a Munich circus, and were inspired (according to Bronnen) to work out what sort of a political show they could put on in a circus themselves. In November the Beer-Cellar Putsch interrupted the rehearsals of *Edward II* for a day. Brecht, with his colleague Bernhard Reich, went to call on Feuchtwanger, who saw this as the sign that they must leave Bavaria (and did in fact leave in 1924). But Reich recalls no particular concern with the Nazis on Brecht's part, and indeed not only was the putsch quite firmly suppressed – and Hitler jailed – but the stabilization of the currency by the Reich government set the Nazi movement back for a number of years.

The years 1918–1924 saw not only a certain element of political restoration throughout central and eastern Europe but also the end of Expressionism in the arts. To the poet-playwright Iwan Goll, who in 1921 published an essay called 'Expressionism is Dying', the two phenomena were connected. 'Expressionism was a fine, good, grand thing . . .' he wrote. 'But the result is, alas, and through no fault of the Expressionists, the German Republic of 1920.' Dadaism likewise was breaking up by 1922; at the Bauhaus the semi-mystical Itten was about to be succeeded by the technologically minded Moholy-Nagy; while artists like Grosz, Dix, Beckmann and Schlichter were evolving the coolly representational, socially conscious style which in 1924 became known as *Neue Sachlichkeit*. Brecht was always much too conscious of his own aims to care to be labelled as part of a movement; none the less his works of these years very clearly reflect the decline of Expressionism and the rise of the new style. He defined his position admirably in a note of 27 June 1920:

> I can compete with the ultra-modernists in hunting for new forms and experimenting with my feelings. But I keep realizing that the essence of art is simplicity, grandeur and sensitivity, and that the essence of its form is coolness.

Baal was written as a kind of counter-play to the Expressionists' invocations of Humanity with a capital H, yet the wandering poet remains a romantic-expressionist figure, while the influence of Georg Büchner is one that is also noticeable in a number of Expressionist plays. *Drums in the Night* too, with its symbolic use of the moon, its cinematic third act and its hero's slightly mad rhetoric, can reasonably be termed an Expressionist play. *In the Jungle*, however, was written at the turning-point, the watershed between the two movements. The Rimbaud allusions, the colour references before each scene in the 1922 version, the attic-cum-undergrowth setting, the use of spotlights referred to in Brecht's note of 1954: all this is expressionistic, whereas the American milieu, the preoccupation with the big cities and the very notion of the 'fight' were to become characteristic concerns of the mid-1920s. A further note of 10 February 1922 even suggests that Brecht was looking forward to his own 1930s doctrine of 'alienation':

> I hope in *Baal* and *Jungle* I've avoided one common artistic bloomer, that of trying to carry people away. Instinctively, I've kept my distance and ensured that the realization of my (poetical and philosophical) effects remains within bounds. The spectator's 'splendid isolation' is left intact; it is not *sua res quae agitur*; he is not fobbed off with an invitation to feel sympathetically, to fuse with the hero and seem significant and indestructible as he watches himself in two different versions. A higher type of interest can be got from making comparisons, from whatever is different, amazing, impossible to overlook.

Thus though *In the Jungle* is still wildly romantic it already foreshadows the detached impersonalities of the machine age. And those supporters who, like Ihering and Engel and Geis, thought that Brecht would help lead the theatre out of the Expressionist undergrowth can now be seen to have been absolutely right.

III

The final texts of these plays often make Brecht's evolution difficult to follow. He was a restless amender and modifier of his own work, so that any one of them may consist of layer upon layer of elements from different periods. 'He is more interested in the job than in the finished work,' wrote Feuchtwanger in an article of 1928 called 'Portrait of Brecht for the English',

> in the problem than in its solution, in the journey than in its goal. He rewrites his works an untold number of times, twenty or thirty times, with a new revision for every minor provincial production. He is not in the least interested in seeing a work completed. . . .

Thus between 1922 and its publication in 1927 *In the Jungle* became *In the Jungle of Cities*. The city allusions were strengthened, the boxing foreword was added and various boxing allusions worked into the text, the colour references at the start of each scene gave way to mock-precise ('objective') data of time and place, the whole flavour of the play was changed. The same was done still more drastically with *Baal* in 1926, though in this case Brecht later decided to scrap the more 'objective', technologically flavoured version and go back (more or less) to the 1922–3 text. *Drums in the Night* he seems to have left alone after 1922, perhaps because it was

not performed again after the first, largely topical wave of interest
had subsided – though the discussion on p. 67 ff. suggests that
Piscator was considering it. Then for his Collected Plays in the
1950s he largely rewrote the last two acts.

All this means that each play as we now have it reflects the views
and to some extent the spirit of a number of different periods. The
performances which have gone into theatrical history were not
based on these particular texts. Even Brecht's own notes are
difficult to understand without knowing to which version each of
them relates.

It is an impossible problem editorially, and our policy has been
to print the final text but to provide all the variant material from
other versions published in Brecht's lifetime, together with extensive notes on the main unpublished scripts. This is so that the
reader should not get false ideas of Brecht's evolution and of his
ideas and achievements at any given time. Brecht was a profound
believer in change, whom it would be wrong to present statically
in a final 'authoritative' mould. Indeed opinions might well differ
as to whether any such mould is the right one: not only are there
fine things in many of the rejected versions, which it would be cruel
not to publish, but informed judgement often disagrees with
Brecht's last choices. Thus the chief German expert on *Baal* and the
author of much the best book on Brecht's early years both prefer
the 1919 script of *Baal*; an outstanding West German theatre critic
wants the 1922 *Drums in the Night*; while Ihering wrote of the (final)
published version of *In the Jungle of Cities* in 1927:

> I love the fullness and colour of the old *Jungle*. There seemed to
> be no better evidence of Brecht's richness and gifts than those
> crackling, exotically pulsating scenes as they shot to and fro. . . .
> The new *Jungle*, the *Jungle of Cities*, has lost in colour and atmo-
> sphere. It has gained in clarity and concentration.

Not that there is much chance that Brecht himself would have
accepted his own choices as final if he had lived longer, or seen
them staged, or looked again at some of the earlier texts which for
one reason or another he did not have before him when preparing
the collected plays. It is characteristic that he already wanted the
1926 version of *Baal* printed as an appendix. For he was always a
man in motion, who progressed best by disagreeing with what had
already been said. Often it had been said by himself.

The German text used throughout, unless otherwise stated, is
that of the *Gesammelte Werke* (or Collected Works) edited by

Elisabeth Hauptmann and a team comprising Werner Hecht, Rosemarie Hill, Herta Ramthun and Klaus Völker, and published by Suhrkamp-Verlag, Frankfurt-am-Main, in 1967. This is referred to as GW, plus the appropriate subdivision: *Stücke* (plays), *Schriften zum Theater* (writings on the theatre), and so on. When the same terms (*Stücke*, for instance), are used without the prefix GW they refer to the earlier collected edition issued by the same publisher from 1953 on. Particulars of other sources are given in full where reference is made to them. We would like to thank the editors and publisher for the help which they have given with various queries. The Brecht Archive in East Berlin has been generous in supplying material, and we are grateful for the support given us from the outset by Stefan S. Brecht.

THE EDITORS

Drums in the Night
a play

Translator: JOHN WILLETT

Characters

Andreas Kragler · Anna Balicke · Karl Balicke, her father ·
Amalie Balicke, her mother · Friedrich Murk, her fiancé ·
Babusch, journalist · Two men · Manke, waiter at the Piccadilly Bar · His brother, waiter at Glubb's bar · Glubb,
schnaps distiller · A drunk man · Bulltrotter, a newspaper
seller · A worker · Laar, a peasant · Augusta, Marie – prosti-
tutes · A maid · A woman selling newspapers

The Manke brothers are played by the same actor.

[*Annotations refer to passages from the 1922 version, printed in the Notes,*
p. 55 ff.]

ACT ONE (AFRICA)

At the Balickes'

Dark room with muslin curtains. Evening.

BALICKE *shaving at the window:* It's now four years since they posted him missing. He'll never come back now. Times are damned uncertain. Any man's worth his weight in gold. I'd have given my blessing two years ago. Your bloody sentimentality stopped me. Nothing'll stop me now.

FRAU BALICKE *by the framed photograph of Kragler as a gunner:* He was such a good man. A man just like a child.

BALICKE: He's dead and buried by now.

FRAU BALICKE: Suppose he comes back.

BALICKE: People don't come back from heaven.

FRAU BALICKE: Anna would drown herself, as heaven's my witness!

BALICKE: If that's what she says she's an ass, and I've never seen an ass drown itself.

FRAU BALICKE: As it is she can't keep anything down.

BALICKE: She shouldn't keep stuffing with blackberries and Bismarck herring. Murk's a fine chap, and we ought to go down on our knees and thank God for him.

FRAU BALICKE: He's making money all right. But compared with *him* . . . It makes me want to cry.

BALICKE: Compared with that corpse? I tell you straight: it's now or never. Is she waiting for the Pope? Has it got to be a nigger? I'm fed up with the whole silly story.

FRAU BALICKE: And suppose he *does* come – the corpse you say is dead and buried – back from heaven or hell? 'The name is Kragler' – who's going to tell him that he's a corpse and his girl is lying in someone else's bed?

BALICKE: I'll tell him. And now *you* tell that creature that I'm fed up and we've ordered the wedding march and it's to be Murk. If *I* tell her she'll flood us out. So kindly put the light on, will you?

FRAU BALICKE: I'll get the sticking plaster. You always cut yourself when there's no light.

BALICKE: Cuts cost nothing, but light . . . *Calls:* Anna!

ANNA *in the doorway:* What is it, Father?

BALICKE: Kindly listen to what your mother's got to say to you and no blubbering on your big day!

FRAU BALICKE: Come over here, Anna. Father thinks you're so pale you can't be sleeping at all.

ANNA: I am sleeping.

FRAU BALICKE: It can't go on like this for ever, don't you see? He'll definitely not come back now. *Lights candles.*

BALICKE: She's making those crocodile eyes again.

FRAU BALICKE: It hasn't been easy for you, and he was such a good man, but he's dead now.

BALICKE: Dead, buried and decayed.

FRAU BALICKE: Karl! And here's Murk, a good hard worker who's sure to get on.

BALICKE: So there you are.

FRAU BALICKE: And you're to say yes, for God's sake.

BALICKE: Without making a song and dance about it.

FRAU BALICKE: You're to accept him, for God's sake.

BALICKE *furiously occupied with his sticking plaster:* Hell and damnation, do you imagine fellows are going to stand being kicked around like footballs? Yes or no! It's rubbish rolling your eyes up to heaven like that.

ANNA: Yes, Father.

BALICKE *huffily:* Blub away, then, the floodgates are open. I'm just off to get my life-jacket.

FRAU BALICKE: Aren't you in love with Murk at all, then?

BALICKE: Well, I call that simply immoral!

FRAU BALICKE: Karl! Well, what about you and Friedrich, Anna?

ANNA: Of course. But of course you know, and I feel so horribly sick.

BALICKE: I know nothing at all! I tell you, the fellow's dead, buried and rotten; all his bones have come apart. Four years! And not a sign of life! And his whole battery blown up! in the air! to smithereens! missing! Not so difficult to say where he has got to, eh? You're too damned scared of ghosts, that's what it is. Get yourself a man, and you won't have to be scared of ghosts any more. *Going up to Anna, expansively.* Are you a brave little woman, or aren't you? Get on with it, then.
Bell rings.

ANNA *frightened:* That's him!

BALICKE: Catch him before he comes in, and put him wise.

FRAU BALICKE *in the door, with the dirty clothes basket:* Haven't you got anything for the laundry?

ANNA: Yes. No. No, I don't think I've got anything . .

FRAU BALICKE: But today's the eighth.

ANNA: The eighth?

FRAU BALICKE: The eighth, of course.

ANNA: And what if it was the eighteenth?

BALICKE: What's all that chatter in the doorway? Come inside.

FRAU BALICKE: Well, you'd better see you have got something for the laundry. *Exit.*

BALICKE *sits down, takes Anna on his knee:* Now look, a woman without a husband, that's a blasphemous business. You've been missing that fellow they sent to a better world, right. But would you know him now? Not a bit of it, my dear. Death has turned him into something fit for a freak show. Three years he's been improving his looks; if he weren't dead as mutton he'd look very different from what you think. Anyway, he's dead and buried and not very pretty. He's got no nose now. But you miss him. So get yourself another man. It's nature, you see. You'll wake up like a dog with two tails. You've got stout limbs and strong appetites, haven't you? That's really not blasphemous, that isn't.

ANNA: But I *can't* forget him. Never. You keep on talking at me, but I *can't*.

BALICKE: You take Murk, he'll help you get over him.

ANNA: I do love him all the same, and one day I'll love him only, but not yet.

BALICKE: He'll bring you round, girl; all he needs is certain prerogatives, the kind of thing that comes best with marriage. I can't explain now, I'll tell you when you're older. *Tickles her.* Well: is that settled?

ANNA *laughs salaciously:* I really don't know if Friedrich wants to.

BALICKE: Mrs, stick your head in.

FRAU BALICKE: Come into the lounge, won't you, Herr Murk, it's an honour.

BALICKE: Evening, Murk. Looking like something out of the morgue, eh?

MURK: Miss Anna!

BALICKE: What's the matter? Bottom fallen out of the market? You're white as a sheet, man. Is it the sound of shooting in the evening air? *Silence.* Come on, Anna, jolly him up.

Exit expansively with his wife.

ANNA: What is it, Friedrich? You really are pale.

MURK *nosing around:* I suppose the red wine's for our engagement? *Silence.* Someone been here? *Going up to Anna.* Anybody been here? Why have you gone so white now? Who's been here?

ANNA: Nobody! No one's been here. What's wrong with you?

MURK: What's the hurry about, then? Don't kid me. Oh, who cares? But I'm not celebrating my engagement in this dump.

ANNA: Who said anything about engagement?

MURK: The old girl. The eye of the Lord maketh the cattle fat. *Walking round restlessly.* Oh well, what about it?

ANNA: You keep acting as if it mattered to my parents. God knows it doesn't matter to my parents. Not the least little bit.

MURK: And when did you leave Sunday school?

ANNA: I just mean you're taking a good deal for granted.

MURK: Really? The other fellow?

ANNA: I wasn't saying anything about the other fellow.

MURK: But there he is, and there he hangs, and there he walks.

ANNA: That was something absolutely different. That was something you'll never understand, because it was spiritual.

MURK: And between you and me, that's carnal?

ANNA: Between you and me, that's nothing.

MURK: What about now? It's something now all right.

ANNA: You don't know anything about it.

MURK: Ha, it'll be a different tune before long.

ANNA: Think what you like.

MURK: I'm asking for your hand.

ANNA: Is that your way of saying you love me?

MURK: That'll come presently.

ANNA: After all, it's a box factory.

MURK: You little tart, you! Didn't they hear anything last night either?

ANNA: Oh, Friedrich! They sleep like dormice! *Snuggles up to him.*

MURK: Not like us.

ANNA: Gangster!

MURK *pulls her to him but kisses her coolly:* Tart!

ANNA: Quiet a moment. That's a train passing in the night. Hear it? Sometimes I'm frightened he's going to turn up. I get shivers all down my back.

MURK: That Egyptian mummy? Leave him to me. Here, let me tell you something: he's got to get out. No stiffs in bed between you and me. I'm not standing for another man in my bed.

ANNA: Don't get annoyed. Will you forgive me, Friedrich?

MURK: Saint Andrew Kragler? Imagination! He'll last as long after our wedding as after his own funeral. Bet on it? *Laughs.* I bet – a baby.

ANNA *hiding her face against him:* Oh, don't say such things, Friedrich.

MURK *stoutly:* Trust me! *To the door.* Come in, Mother. Evening, Father.

FRAU BALICKE *immediately behind the door:* Oh, children! *Bursts into tears.* What a wonderful surprise!

BALICKE: Difficult birth, what? *Mutual embraces and emotion.*

MURK: Triplets! When shall we have the wedding? Time's money.

BALICKE: Three weeks would suit me. The twin beds are in good shape. Supper, Mother!

FRAU BALICKE: In a moment, in a moment, just let me get my breath. *Hurrying out.* What a wonderful surprise!

MURK: May I have the pleasure of inviting you to split a bottle with me at the Piccadilly Bar tonight? I'm for celebrating our engagement right away, aren't you, Anna?

ANNA: If we must.

BALICKE: Here, though. Why the Piccadilly Bar? Are you in your right mind?

MURK *uneasily:* Not here. Definitely not here.

BALICKE: Well, what next?

ANNA: He's funny. So come along to the Piccadilly Bar, then.

BALICKE: Tonight of all nights! At the risk of one's life!

FRAU BALICKE *enters with the maid, bringing supper:* Here you are, children. Everything comes to him who waits. Take your places, gentlemen.

They stuff.

BALICKE *raises his glass:* To the happy pair! *Clinking glasses.* Times are uncertain. The war's over. This pork is too fatty, Amalie. Now the demobilization's washing greed, disorder and swinish inhumanity into the still backwaters of peaceful labour.

MURK: Where we turn out ammunition boxes, cheers! Cheers, Anna!

BALICKE: Doubtful characters appearing on the scene, shady gentlemen. The government's being far too soft with

those scavengers of the revolution. *Opens a newspaper.* The masses are all worked up and without any ideals. And worst of all – I can say it here – the troops back from the front, shabby, half-savage adventurers who've lost the habit of working and hold nothing sacred. Truly a difficult time, Anna, a man's worth his weight in gold. Hold on to him. It'll be up to you two to win through, but always as a couple, mind you, always winning through, cheers!
He winds up a gramophone.

MURK *wiping away perspiration:* Bravo! You've got to be a man to come through. You want a pair of elbows and nails in your boots, and the right looks and no backward glances. What's to stop us, Anna? I'm from the bottom myself. Errand boy, shop floor, a turn of the hand here and there, picked up a thing or two. The whole of Germany's worked its way up like that. Not with kid gloves on always, but hard work the whole time, God knows! Now on top! Cheers, Anna! *The gramophone plays 'Ich bete an die Macht der Liebe'.*

BALICKE: Bravo! Well, what's wrong, Anna?

ANNA *has got up, stands half turned away:* I don't know. It's all happening so quickly. Perhaps that isn't a good thing, eh, Mother?

FRAU BALICKE: What's the matter, child? So silly! Go on, enjoy yourself. Not a good thing, indeed!

BALICKE: Sit! Or wind the gramophone, as you're up.
Anna sits down.
Pause.

MURK: So cheers, then! *Clinks glasses with Anna.* What's wrong?

BALICKE: Then about the business, Fritz, ammunition boxes, that'll soon be a dead duck. A few more weeks of civil war, that's the best you can hope for, then finish. I know the ideal answer, I'm not joking: children's prams. The factory's tip-top all along the line. *He takes Murk's arm and draws him upstage. Pulls back the curtains.* New buildings Three and Four. All modern and permanent. Anna, wind up the gramophone. I always find that moving. *The gramophone plays 'Deutschland, Deutschland über alles'.*

MURK: Hey, there's a man in the factory yard. What's going on?

ANNA: Oh, how creepy! I think he's looking up here.

BALICKE: Probably the night-watchman. Why are you laughing, Fritz! Cough it up. The ladies look quite pale.

MURK: A funny idea came into my head: the Spartacists, don't you know . . .

BALICKE: Rubbish. None of that round here. *Turns away all the same, disagreeably disturbed.* So that's the factory. *Approaches the table. Anna draws the curtain.* The war put me in the proverbial clover. The stuff was lying around for anybody to pick up, why not, it would have been too stupid. Someone else would have had it. Can't make omelettes without breaking eggs. Looked at the right way the war was a godsend to us. We've got our pile, round, fat, and snug. We can sit back and make prams. No special hurry. Am I right?

MURK: Absolutely, Dad. Cheers!

BALICKE: The same way you can sit back and make children. Hahahaha.

MAID: Herr Babusch, Herr Balicke.

BABUSCH *trots in:* Hey, hey, you folks are well dug in against the red terror. Spartacus has mobilized. Negotiations been broken off. Artillery fire over Berlin in another twenty-four hours.

BALICKE *has his napkin round his neck:* To hell with it, can't those fellows be satisfied?

FRAU BALICKE: Artillery? O godogodogodogod! What a night! What a night! Balicke, I'm going to the cellar.

BABUSCH: It's all quiet so far in the central districts.[1] But the story is that they want to seize the newspaper offices.

BALICKE: What! We're celebrating an engagement! And this is the day we choose! Quite mad!

MURK: They should execute the lot.

BALICKE: A firing squad for all grumblers.

BABUSCH: Is it *your* engagement, Balicke?

MURK: Babusch: my fiancée.

FRAU BALICKE: A wonderful surprise. But when'll the shooting start?

BABUSCH *shakes Anna's and Murk's hands:* Spartacus have been hoarding weapons for all they're worth. Lowdown secretive lot. Anna, Anna! Don't let them put you off. Nothing'll touch you here. Here's a peaceful retreat. The family. The German family. My home is my castle.

FRAU BALICKE: What times these are! What times these are! And on your big day! Anna!

BABUSCH: It's damned interesting all the same, folks.

BALICKE: Not to me it isn't. Not one little bit. *Wipes his mouth with the napkin.*

MURK: You know what? Come to the Piccadilly Bar with us. We're celebrating.

BABUSCH: And Spartacus?

BALICKE: Can wait, Babusch. Shoot some other fellow in the guts, Babusch. Come to the Piccadilly Bar with us. Get your fineries on, girls!

FRAU BALICKE: Piccadilly Bar? Tonight? *Sits on a chair.*

BALICKE: Piccadilly Bar it used to be called. It's the Café Vaterland now. Friedrich's taking us out. What's wrong with tonight? What are cabs for? Gee up; get your togs on, old girl!

FRAU BALICKE: I'm not moving a foot outside these four walls. What's got into you, Fritzi?

ANNA: It's a free country. Friedrich seems to want it. *All look at Murk.*

MURK: Not here. Definitely not here. Me, I want music, lights. It's a classy place. Here it's all dark. I put my decent outfit on on purpose. So how about it, Mother?

FRAU BALICKE: It's all beyond me. *Leaves the room.*

ANNA: Wait for me, Friedrich, I'll be ready in a minute.

BABUSCH: Lots happening, boys. The whole bag of tricks is going up. Babes in arms, get yourselves organized! By the way, apricots, soft as butter, flesh-coloured, juicy, are five marks the pound. Loafers, don't let them provoke you! Everywhere shady gangs are sticking their fingers in their mouths and whistling into the brightly lit cafés. Their emblem, the idle loaf. And the dance-halls full of the so-called upper crust. Well, here's to your wedding-day!

MURK: The ladies aren't changing. We're all equal now. Too much dazzle only makes you conspicuous.

BALICKE: Hear hear. Critical time like this. Any old outfit's good enough for this shower. Come down at once, Anna.

MURK: We're going straight on. Don't change.

ANNA: Roughneck! *Exit.*

BALICKE: Gee up ... Sound the trumpets, next stop paradise. I must change my shirt.

MURK: You'll follow on with Mother, eh? And Babusch can come with us, and be our chaperone, eh? *Sings.* Babusch, Babusch, Babusch, trotting to and fro.

BABUSCH: That miserable third-rate, crazy schoolboy doggerel, can't you forget it? *Exit, taking his arm.*

MURK *still singing off:* Pull your finger out, my lads, and make the party go. Anna!

BALICKE *alone, lights a cigar:* Thank God for that. All snug as a bug. What a damn grind! You have to drive her to bed. Calf love for that corpse! My clean shirt's soaked with sweat. Now I can take them all on. Pram's the word. *Exit.* Mrs, a shirt!

ANNA *off:* Friedrich! Friedrich! *Enter quickly.* Friedrich!

MURK *in the doorway:* Anna! *Dry, uneasy, with hanging arms like an orang-outang.* Do you want to come along?

ANNA: What's the matter? What are you looking like that for?

MURK: Do you want to come? I know what I'm asking. Don't play-act. Straight answer!

ANNA: I should think I do. Odd, isn't it?

MURK: Fine, then. I'm not so sure. Twenty years I lodged in attics, frozen to the marrow; now I wear buttoned boots, look for yourself! I sweated in the darkness, by gaslight, it ran into my eyes; now I go to a tailor. But I'm still unsteady, the wind blows down there, there's an icy draught down there, one's feet get chilled down there. *Goes up to Anna without touching her, stands swaying in front of her.* At last the superfluous flesh is increasing. At last the red wine is flowing. At last I've got there! Bathed in sweat, eyes shut, fists clenched till the fingernails cut into the flesh. It's over! Security! Warmth! Off with the overalls! A bed, white, broad, soft! *As he passes the window he glances fleetingly out.* Come to me: I'll unclench my fists, I'll sit in the sun in my shirtsleeves, I've got you.

ANNA *flies to him:* Darling!

MURK: Sex kitten!

ANNA: At last you've got me.

MURK: Isn't she there yet?

BABUSCH *off:* Come on, come on! I'm the bridesmaid, folks.

MURK *winds the gramophone once more. It again starts 'Ich bete an die Macht der Liebe':* I'm the best possible fellow if only they'll give me my head. *Exeunt both, in close contact with each other.*

FRAU BALICKE *swishes in, in black, arranges her bonnet in front of the glass:* Such a huge moon and so red ... And the children, dear God! Yes, yes ... we've much to be thankful for in our prayers tonight.

At this point a man with a muddy dark blue artillery uniform and a stumpy pipe appears in the door.

THE MAN: The name is Kragler.

FRAU BALICKE *supports herself, with trembling knees, against the table the mirror is on:* Good heav ...

KRAGLER: Well, no need to look so supernatural. Did *you* chuck away good money on a wreath too? Pity. Beg to report: set up shop as a ghost in Algiers. But now the corpse is most horribly hungry. I could eat worms. What's the matter, Ma Balicke? Idiotic song! *Stops the gramophone. Frau Balicke continues to say nothing and simply stares at him.*

KRAGLER: Don't faint all at once. Here's a chair. There ought to be a glass of water about. *Goes humming to the cupboard.* Still know my way around pretty well. *Pours wine.*

Wine! Nierensteiner! Plenty of life in the old ghost, eh?
Sees to Frau Balicke.

BALICKE *off:* Come along, old girl! On the move! How
beautiful you are, my angel! *Comes in, stands taken aback.*
Well?

KRAGLER: Evening, Herr Balicke. Your wife's not feeling
well. *Tries to make her drink some wine, but she turns away in
horror.*
Balicke looks on uncomfortably for a moment.

KRAGLER: Won't you have some? You won't? It'll pass in a
moment. No idea I was so fresh in the memory. Just back
from Africa, you see. Spain, fiddle with passports, and all
the rest of it. But where's Anna?

BALICKE: Leave my wife alone, for God's sake. You're
drowning her.

KRAGLER: As you say.

FRAU BALICKE *takes refuge with Balicke, who stands upright:*
Karl!

BALICKE *severely:* Herr Kragler, if you are the person you
claim to be, would you mind telling me what you are doing
here?

KRAGLER *shocked:* You realize I was a prisoner of war in
Africa?

BALICKE: Hell! *Goes to a small cupboard, drinks a schnaps.*
That's fine. You would be. A damned disgusting business!
What d'you want? My daughter announced her engage-
ment less than half an hour ago.

KRAGLER *staggers, a bit unsure:* What do you mean?

BALICKE: You've been away four years. She's waited four
years. We've waited four years. Now time's up and you've
had your chance.
Kragler sits down.

BALICKE *not quite firmly, unsure but making an effort to preserve
his dignity:* Herr Kragler, I have commitments this evening.

KRAGLER *looking up:* Commitments . . . ? *Distractedly.* Yes . . .
Slumps back.

FRAU BALICKE: Don't take it too hard, Herr Kragler. There

are lots of other girls. That's the way it is. You must grin and bear it.

KRAGLER: Anna!

BALICKE *curtly:* Mrs! *She goes hesitantly to him, he suddenly firm:* Bah! Sentimental stuff, let's go. *Exit with his wife. The maid appears in the door.*

KRAGLER: Hm! . . . *Shakes his head.*

MAID: Herr and Frau Balicke have gone out.
Silence.
Herr and Frau Balicke have gone to the Piccadilly Bar for the engagement party.
Silence. Wind.

KRAGLER *looking up at her:* Hm! *He gets up slowly and laboriously, looks round the room. Walks around silently, with bent head, looks through the window, turns round, slowly takes himself off, whistling, without his cap.*

MAID: Here! Your cap! You've left your cap behind!

ACT TWO (PEPPER)

Piccadilly Bar

Big window at the back. Music. In the window a red moon. When the door opens, wind.

BABUSCH: This way to the menagerie, folks! There's plenty of moonlight. Up Spartacus! Bullshit! Red wine!

MURK *enters with Anna on his arm, they take off their things:* A night like in a story-book. Shouting round the newspaper offices. The coach bearing the happy couple.

ANNA: It's no good, I feel horrible today. I can't control my arms and legs.

BABUSCH: Cheers to that, Friedrich!

MURK: This is where I'm at home. Damned uncomfortable in the long run but absolutely slap-up. Look after the older generation, will you, Babusch?

BABUSCH: Right. *Drinks.* You look after the next. *Goes out.*

ANNA: Kiss me.

MURK: Nonsense. Half Berlin's looking.

ANNA: Doesn't matter. Nothing matters when I want something. Don't you find that?

MURK: Not for a minute. Nor do you.

ANNA: You're common.

MURK: That's right.

ANNA: Coward! *Murk rings, enter a waiter.*

MURK: Atten . . . shun! *He leans across the table, knocking glasses over, and forcibly kisses Anna.*

ANNA: You!

MURK: Dis . . . miss! *Exit waiter.* Am I a coward? *Looks under the table.* And you needn't push your feet at me now.

ANNA: What's got into you?

MURK: Honour and obey, that's it.

BALICKE *enters with Babusch and Frau Balicke:* There they are.
   Service!

ANNA: Where've you been?

FRAU BALICKE: There's such a red moon tonight. I'm quite
   upset because it's so red. And more shouting round the
   newspaper offices.

BABUSCH: Pack of wolves.

FRAU BALICKE: See that you two get together.

BALICKE: In bed, Friedrich, eh?

ANNA: Mother, are you all right?

FRAU BALICKE: When do you think of getting married?

MURK: In three weeks, Mamma.

FRAU BALICKE: Shouldn't we have asked more people to
   come and celebrate? This way nobody knows. But they
   ought to know.

BALICKE: Rubbish, I say, rubbish. Because the wolves are
   howling? Let them howl. Till their tongue hangs red
   between their knees. I'll shoot them down, no question.

BABUSCH: Murk, help me get the cork out. *Quietly to him:*
   He's there. Arrived with the moon. The wolf with the
   moon. From Africa.

MURK: Andy Kragler?

BABUSCH: The wolf. Not funny, is it?

MURK: He's in his grave, that's all. Pull the curtains.

FRAU BALICKE: Every other doorway your father found a
   boozer to tumble into. He's got a monkey on his back all
   right. There's a man for you! What a man! He'll drink
   himself to death for his children, that man will.

ANNA: Yes, but what makes him do it?

FRAU BALICKE: Don't ask, child. Don't ask me. Everything's upside down. The world's coming to an end. I must
   have a kirsch at once, child.

BALICKE: That's only the red moon, Mother. Draw the curtains! *Waiter does so.*

BABUSCH: You had a hunch?

MURK: I'm ready down to the last button. Has he been to
   their place?

BABUSCH: Yes, just now.

MURK: Then he'll come here.

BALICKE: What are you two cooking behind the bottles? Park yourselves here! Engagement party! *All sit around the table.* Get cracking! I haven't time to feel tired.

ANNA: Ha, the horse! Wasn't that funny? The middle of the road, and he just stopped. Friedrich, get out, the horse has packed up. And then in the middle of the road the horse standing. And trembling. It had eyeballs like gooseberries, though, all white, and Friedrich prodded its eyes with a stick and made it hop. It was like a circus.

BALICKE: Time's money. It's damned hot here. I'm sweating again. I've sweated one shirt through today already.

FRAU BALICKE: You'll land us in the workhouse with the laundry bills, the way things are going.

BABUSCH *munching prunes from his pocket:* Apricots are ten marks a pound now. Well, well. I shall write an article about prices. Then I'll be able to buy apricots. Suppose the world does come to an end, I'll write about it. But what are the others to do? If the whole Zoo district blows up I'll be sitting pretty. But the people . . .!

MURK: Shirts, apricots, the Zoo. When's the wedding?

BALICKE: In three weeks. Wedding in three weeks' time. I have spoken. Heaven has heard it. We all agreed? All agreed about the wedding? Right, then ready, steady, go, the happy couple! *They clink glasses. The door has opened. Kragler stands in the doorway. The wind makes the candles flicker and dim.*

BALICKE: Now, now, why so shaky with the glass? Like your mother, Anna?

Anna, who is sitting opposite the door, has seen Kragler. She sits hunched up and looks fixedly at him.

FRAU BALICKE: Good heavens, what's made you fold up like that, child?

MURK: What's that wind?

KRAGLER *hoarsely:* Anna!

Anna gives a subdued scream. All now look round, leap to their feet. Tumult. Speaking at once:

BALICKE: Hell! *Pours wine down his gullet.* The ghost, Mother!

FRAU BALICKE: God! Kra . . .

MURK: Throw him out! Throw him out!

Kragler has remained swaying in the doorway for a moment; he looks sinister. During the short tumult he comes quite quickly but clumsily up to Anna, who is now sitting alone holding her glass shakily before her face, takes the glass away from her, props himself on the table, and stares at her.

BALICKE: He's drunk.

MURK: Waiter! This is a disturbance of the peace. Throw him out! *Runs along the wall, pulls back the curtain in the process. Moon.*

BABUSCH: Be careful. He's got raw flesh under his shirt still. It's stinging him. Don't touch him. *Bangs the table with his stick.* No scenes here, please. Leave quietly. Pull yourselves together and leave.

ANNA *has meanwhile left the table and throws her arms round her mother:* Mother! Help!

Kragler goes round the table unsteadily after Anna.

FRAU BALICKE *all more or less simultaneously:* Spare my child's life! You'll end up in gaol! Oh God, he's killing her!

BALICKE *at a considerable distance, swelling up:* Are you drunk? Pauper! Anarchist! Ex-serviceman! You pirate! You moon ghost! Where's your white sheet?

BABUSCH: If you have a stroke now he'll marry her. Shut up, all of you! He's the one who's been wronged. Clear out! He must be allowed to have his say. He has a right to. *To Frau Balicke:* Haven't you any feeling? Four years he's been away. It's a matter of feeling.

FRAU BALICKE: She can hardly stand on her legs, she's as white as chalk.

BABUSCH *to Murk:* Have a look at his face. She's seen it already. It used to be like milk and blood. Now it's a rotten lemon. No need for you to be frightened. *Exeunt.*

MURK: If you're thinking about jealousy I'm not that sort. Ha!

BALICKE *is still standing between the door and the table, somewhat*

*drunk, with crooked legs and a glass in his hand. During what
follows he says:* That wog on wheels! Face like a, a collapsed
elephant. Utterly broken down. A piece of impertinence.
*Clears off so that there's now nobody left but the waiter by the door
right, a tray in his hands. Gounod's 'Ave Maria'. The light goes
down.*

KRAGLER *after a moment:* It's as if everything in my head had
been wiped away, I've nothing but sweat left there, I find it
hard to understand things.

ANNA *picks up a candle, stands helplessly, lights up his face:* Didn't
the fishes eat you?

KRAGLER: I don't know what you mean.

ANNA: Weren't you blown to pieces?

KRAGLER: I can't understand you.

ANNA: Didn't they shoot your face away?

KRAGLER: Why are you looking at me like that? Is that what
I look like? *Silence. He looks towards the window.* I've a skin
like a shark's: black. *Silence.* And I used to be like milk and
blood. *Silence.* And then I keep on bleeding, it just streams
out of me.

ANNA: Andy.

KRAGLER: Yes.

ANNA *going hesitantly towards him:* Oh, Andy, why were
you away so long? Did they bar your way with guns
and swords? And now I can no longer get through to
you.

KRAGLER: Was I away?

ANNA: You were with me a long while at the beginning, your
voice hadn't yet died away. When I walked down the passage I brushed against you and in the fields I heard you calling from behind the sycamore. Even though they wrote
that your face had been shot away and two days later you'd
been buried. But the time came when it changed. When I
walked down the passage, it was deserted, and the sycamore
had nothing to say. When I straightened myself over the
washtub I could still see your face, but when I spread the
things on the grass I lost sight of it and all that long while

I had no idea what you looked like. But I ought to have waited.

KRAGLER: You could have done with a photo.

ANNA: I was frightened. I ought to have waited all the same, but I am no good. Don't touch my hand, nothing about me's any good.

KRAGLER *looks towards the window:* I don't know what you're talking about. Perhaps it's just the red moon. I must try and think what it means. I've got swollen hands, they've got webs on them, I've no manners and I break glasses when I drink. I can't talk properly to you any longer. My throat's full of nigger language.

ANNA: Yes.

KRAGLER: Give me your hand. Do you think I'm a ghost? Come here, give me your hand. Don't you want to come to me?

ANNA: Do you want it?

KRAGLER: Give it me. I've stopped being a ghost now. Can you see my face again? Is it like crocodile hide? I can't see properly. I've been in salty water. It's just the red moon.

ANNA: Yes.

KRAGLER: You take my hand too. – Why don't you press it? Give me your face. Is it bad?

ANNA: No, no.

KRAGLER *takes hold of her:* Anna! A wog on wheels, that's me. Throat full of crap. Four years! Will you have me? Anna! *Pulls her round and catches sight of the waiter, whom he stares at with a grin while bending forward.*

WAITER *disconcerted, drops his tray, stammers:* The point is . . . her lily . . . has she still got her lily?

KRAGLER *with his hands round Anna, gives a horse-laugh:* What did he say? Lily? *The waiter hurries off.* Here, wait a moment, you with the taste for cheap novels. That's something he didn't mean to say. Lily! Something that's happened to him. Lily! Did you hear it? He felt it as deeply as that.

ANNA: Andy!

KRAGLER *looks at her, stooping, having let go of her:* Say that again, that's your voice. *Hurries off right.* Waiter! Come here, man.

BABUSCH *in the doorway:* What a fleshly laugh you have. You laugh velly fleshly. How's it going?

FRAU BALICKE *behind him:* Anna, my child! What a worry you are to us! *Next door 'The Lady from Peru' has been playing for a while.*

BALICKE *sobered up somewhat, hurries in:* Sit down. *He draws the curtain, there is a metallic sound.* They've got the red moon with them and rifles behind them in Babusch's newspaper district. They're a serious proposition. *He relights all the candles.* Sit down.

FRAU BALICKE: What a look on your face! My legs are starting to shake again. Waiter! Waiter!

BALICKE: Where's Murk?

BABUSCH: Friedrich Murk's shuffling round the dance floor.

BALICKE *softly:* Just get him to sit down. Once he's sitting we can get him where we want him. Nobody can make a drama sitting down. *Aloud.* Sit down, everybody. Quiet! Pull yourself together, Amalie. *To Kragler:* You sit down too, for God's sake.

FRAU BALICKE *takes a bottle of kirsch from the waiter's tray:* I've got to have kirsch or I'll die. *She returns to the table with it.*

The following are seated: Frau Balicke, Balicke, Anna. Babusch has leapt around and got them to sit down. He now pushes Kragler, who was standing looking lost, into a chair.

BABUSCH: Sit down, your knees aren't too firm. Would you like some kirsch? Why do you laugh like that? *Kragler gets up again. Babusch pushes him down. He remains seated.*

BALICKE: Andreas Kragler, what do you want?

FRAU BALICKE: Herr Kragler! Our Kaiser said, 'You must grin and bear it.'

ANNA: Stay in your chair.

BALICKE: Shut up! Let him speak. What do you want?

BABUSCH *rises:* Would you like a nip of kirsch perhaps? Speak up!

ANNA: Think, Andy. Before you say anything.

FRAU BALICKE: You'll have me in my grave. Hold your tongue! You don't understand a thing.

KRAGLER *wants to get up, but is pushed back by Babusch. With extreme seriousness:* If you're asking me it's not at all simple. And I don't want to drink any kirsch. There's too much involved.

BALICKE: Get a move on. Say what you want. Then I'll chuck you out.

ANNA: No, no!

BABUSCH: You'd better have a drink, you know. You're so dried up. It'll make it easier, believe me. *At this point Friedrich Murk shuffles in left with a prostitute called Marie.*

FRAU BALICKE: Murk!

BABUSCH: Genius has its limits. Sit down.

BALICKE: Bravo, Fritz! Show the man what a man's made of! Fritz isn't scared. Fritz is having fun. *Claps.*

MURK *sinister, he has been drinking, leaves Marie standing where she is and comes to the table:* Haven't you settled this third-rate farce yet?

BALICKE *pulls him down on to a chair:* Shut up!

BABUSCH: Go on, Kragler. Ignore interruptions.

KRAGLER: He's got misshapen ears.

ANNA: He used to be the look-out boy.

MURK: He's got an egg in his noddle.

KRAGLER: He must leave the room!

MURK: Then they hit him on it.

KRAGLER: I must be very careful what I say.

MURK: So he's got egg-nog in his noddle.

KRAGLER: Yes, they hit me on the head. I've been away four years. I couldn't write letters. There was no egg in my brain. *Silence.* Four years have passed, I must be very careful. You (*Anna*) haven't recognized me, you're still on a see-saw and can't feel it yet. But I'm talking too much.

FRAU BALICKE: His brains have dried up. *Shaking her head.*

BALICKE: Had a bad time did you? Fought for Kaiser and Country? I feel sorry for you. Anything you want?

FRAU BALICKE: And the Kaiser said, 'Be strong in your sorrow.' Have some of this. *Pushes the kirsch towards him.*

BALICKE *drinking, weightily:* You stood under a hail of bullets? Firm as a rock? Splendid. Our army can be proud of itself. It marched to a hero's death with a song on its lips. Have a drink. What do you want?

ANNA: Andy! Didn't they give you another uniform? Still got the old blue one on? Those aren't worn any more.

FRAU BALICKE: There are lots of other girls! Waiter, more kirsch! *Passes him the kirsch.*

BALICKE: We did our bit too. So what do you want? Not a penny to your name? No place of your own? Fatherland can only offer you a barrel-organ? We can't have that. That kind of thing can't be allowed to happen any longer. What do you want?

ANNA: 'Stormy the night and the sea runs high,' ha!

KRAGLER *has risen. To Anna:* Since I feel I've no rights here I beg you, from the bottom of my heart, to go with me at my side.

BALICKE: What kind of talk is that? What's he saying? Bottom of my heart. At my side. What an extraordinary way of speaking.
The others laugh.

KRAGLER: Because no one's got a right . . . Because I can't live without you . . . From the bottom of my heart.
Much laughter.

MURK *puts his feet up on the table. Cold, nasty, drunk:* Sunk right to the ocean bed. Fished up. Mouth full of slime. Look at my boots. They used to be the same sort as yours. Buy yourself a pair like mine. Come again. Do you know what you are?

MARIE *suddenly:* Were you in the army?

WAITER: Were you in the army?

MURK: Shut your trap! *To Kragler:* The steamroller squashed you, did it? The steamroller squashed a lot of people. All right. It wasn't us set it rolling. Got no face left? Eh? Want a new one for nothing? Are the three of us supposed to fit you out again? Was it because of us you went under? Do you still not know what you are?

BABUSCH: Oh, do be quiet.

WAITER *coming forward:* Were you in the army?

MURK: Nope. I'm one of the people who have to settle the bill for your heroism. The roller's gone bust.

BABUSCH: Oh, don't make a drama of this. It's too squalid. After all, you made a packet, didn't you? So leave your boots out of it.

BALICKE: There you are, that's the long and the short of it. That's where the shoe pinches. It isn't a drama. It's political realism. Something we Germans are short of. It's very simple. Have you got the means to support a wife? Or have you got webbed fingers?

FRAU BALICKE: Hear that, Anna? He hasn't a penny.

MURK: If he has I'll marry his mother. *Jumps up.* He's just a perfectly ordinary fortune-hunter.

WAITER *to Kragler:* Say something! Answer something!

KRAGLER *has risen, trembling, to Anna:* I don't know what to say. When we were just skin and bone, and we kept having to drink schnaps to be able to work on the roads, we'd often only the evening sky, that's extremely important, because that's when I lay in the bushes with you in April. I used to say the same thing to the others. But they went down like flies.

ANNA: Like horses, no?

KRAGLER: Because of the heat, and we kept boozing away. But why am I going on telling you about the evening sky, that's not what I meant to do, I don't know . . .

ANNA: Were you always thinking of me?

FRAU BALICKE: Listen to his way of speaking! Like a child. Makes you blush for him, to hear it.

MURK: Won't you sell me your boots? For the war museum. I'll offer forty marks.

BABUSCH: Go on speaking, Kragler. It's just what's needed.

KRAGLER: Then we didn't have any shirts left. That was the

worst of all, I can tell you. Can you conceive that that might be the worst of all?

ANNA: Andy, they're listening to you.

MURK: Then I offer sixty marks. You ought to sell.

KRAGLER: Beginning to be ashamed of me, are you? Because they're standing round the ring like in a circus and the elephant's pissing with fear. Yet they know absolutely nothing.

MURK: Eighty marks.

KRAGLER: I'm not a pirate. The red moon's no affair of mine. It's just that I can't get my eyes open. I'm flesh and blood and I've got a clean shirt on. So I'm not a ghost.

MURK *leaps up:* A hundred marks, then.

MARIE: You should be ashamed to the depths of your soul.

MURK: The swine, he won't let me have his old boots for a hundred marks.

KRAGLER: Something's speaking, Anna. What's that voice?

MURK: You've got sunstroke. Do you need help to leave?

KRAGLER: Anna, it thinks it shouldn't be squashed.

MURK: Are we seeing your face at last?

KRAGLER: Anna, it's one of God's creatures.

MURK: Is that you? What do you really want? You're just a corpse. You're getting smelly. *Holds his nose.* Have you no idea of hygiene? D'you want a monument put up to you because you've had a touch of the African sun? I've worked. I've sweated till the blood ran into my boots. Look at my hands. You get all the sympathy, because you got yourself shot up, it wasn't me did the shooting. You're a hero and I'm a worker. And that's my girl.

BABUSCH: That still holds good if you sit down, Murk. You're still a worker sitting down. Kragler, the history of humanity would be different if only people sat on their bottoms more.

KRAGLER: I can't see into him. He's like a lavatory wall. Covered with obscene scribbles. Not the wall's fault. Anna, is that the man you love? Is it?

Anna laughs and drinks.

BABUSCH: You're cutting off your nose to spite your face, Kragler.

KRAGLER: I'm cutting out a tumour. Is it him you love? With a green face like an unripe nut? Am I to be sent away for his sake? He's got an English suit and a chest padded out with paper and boots full of blood. And I have only my old suit, which has the moth in it. Say you can't marry me because of my suit, say it. I'd rather!

BABUSCH: Oh, do sit down. To hell with it. Now we're off.

MARIE: That's him! And the embarrassing way he danced with me, how he pushed his knees into my stomach.

MURK: Put a cork in it. They only have to look at you. Haven't you got a knife on you that you can cut my throat with, because you got bubbles in the brain in Africa? Get out your knife, I'm fed up to here, slit it through.

FRAU BALICKE: How can you listen, Anna?

BALICKE: Waiter, bring me four glasses of kirsch. I couldn't care less.

MURK: Mind you don't draw that knife. Pull yourself together, we don't want you playing the hero here. Here it means gaol.

MARIE: Were you in the army?

MURK *furious, chucks a glass at her*: Why weren't you?

KRAGLER: At last I've come.

MURK: Who asked you?

KRAGLER: At last I've got there.

MURK: Swine!

ANNA: Don't answer.

Kragler lets it pass.

MURK: Bandit!

KRAGLER *silently*: Thief!

MURK: Ghost!

KRAGLER: Look out.

MURK: You look out for that knife of yours. Feel it twitching? Ghost! Ghost! Ghost!

MARIE: You swine! You swine!

KRAGLER: Anna! Anna! What am I doing? Staggering over

the ocean full of corpses: it won't drown *me*. Rolling south in darkened cattle-trucks: nothing can happen to *me*. Burning in the fiery furnace: I myself burn hotter. Someone goes mad in the sun: not me, thank you. Two men fall down a water-hole: I sleep on. I shoot niggers. I eat grass. I'm a ghost. *At this point the waiter rushes to the window and pulls the curtain. The music stops abruptly, there are excited cries of They're coming! Quiet! The waiter blows out the candles.* [2] *> Sound of the 'Internationale' from outside. <* [2]

A MAN *appears in the door left:* Ladies and gentlemen, please keep calm. You are requested not to leave the premises. Disturbances have broken out. They are fighting around the newspaper offices. The outcome is uncertain.

BALICKE *sits down heavily:* Spartacus! Your friends, Mr Andreas Kragler. Your murky companions. Your comrades who are now roaring round the newspaper offices.[3] Smelling of murder and arson. Animals! *Silence.* Animals! Animals! Animals! Want to know why you're animals: you eat flesh. You should be stamped out.

WAITER: By you! You who've eaten yourselves silly!

MURK: Where d'you keep your knife! Out with it!

MARIE *goes up to him with the waiter:* Will you shut up?

WAITER: It's inhuman. Animal, that's what it is.

MURK: Draw the curtains! Ghosts!

WAITER: Are we supposed to be put up against a wall we built with our own hands, while you people swill down kirsch behind it?

KRAGLER: There's my hand and there's my artery. Cut it. If I'm destroyed it'll bleed all right.

MURK: Ghost! Ghost! What are you really? Am I supposed to grovel because you've got an African skin on?[4] And go roaring round the newspaper offices? Is it my fault you were in Africa? Is it my fault I wasn't?

WAITER: He must get his girl back. It's inhuman.

FRAU BALICKE *in front of Anna, furiously:* The whole lot are sick. They've all got something. Syphilis! Syphilis! They've all got syphilis!

BABUSCH *bangs the table with his stick:* That's the last straw.

FRAU BALICKE: Kindly leave my child alone! Kindly leave her alone! You hycna! You're a swine, you are!

ANNA: Andy, I can't. You people are destroying me.

MARIE: You're the swine.

WAITER: It's not human. A man must have some rights.

FRAU BALICKE: Be quiet! You menial! You little bastard, I ordered kirsch, do you hear? You'll be sacked!

WAITER: It's the human element. It's all of our business. He must get . . .

KRAGLER: Oh, get out. I've had enough. Human and inhuman! What does that drunk cow think she wants? I've been on my own and I want my girl. What does that sodden archangel think he wants? D'you want to hawk her body as if it were a pound of coffee? Tear her away from me with grappling-hooks and you'll simply rip her apart.

WAITER: You'll rip her apart.

MARIE: Yes, like a pound of coffee.

BALICKE: A man absolutely without money!

BABUSCH: You kick his teeth in, he spits them back in your face.

MURK *to Anna:* You look like a baby's vomit, letting him lick you up with his eyes like that. With a face like you'd pissed in a bed of nettles.

BALICKE: Is that how you speak about your fiancée?

MURK: Fiancée! That what she is? My fiancée, is she? Isn't she cutting loose already? Back, is he? Do you love him? Is the unripe nut sinking to the bottom? Is it African thighs you've an urge for? Is that the way the wind lies?

BABUSCH: That's something you wouldn't have said if you'd been sitting down.

ANNA *continually getting closer to Kragler, regards Murk with disgust. Softly:* You're drunk.

MURK *pulls her to him:* Let's see your face! Show us your teeth! Whore!

KRAGLER *simply lifts Murk to his feet, the glasses rattle on the table, Marie keeps applauding:* You're not too steady on your feet. Go outside. Make yourself sick. You've drunk too much. You're falling over. *Gives him a push.*

MARIE: Let him have it! Do let him have it!

KRAGLER: Leave him be. Come to me, Anna. I want you now. He wanted to buy my boots off me, but I'm taking my coat off. The sleet cut through my skin so that it's red and splits in the sun. My bag's empty, I have no money whatever, I want you. I'm not beautiful. Up to now I've been frightened out of my wits, but now I'm drinking. *Drinks.* And then we'll go. Come!

MURK *completely collapsed, tipped towards Kragler, says almost calmly:* Don't drink. You don't know the half of it. Call it a day. I was drunk. But you don't know the half of it. Anna – *soberly* – you tell him. What are you going to do? In your state?

KRAGLER *doesn't hear him:* Don't be frightened, Anna! *With the kirsch.* Nothing will happen to you. No call to be scared. We'll get married. I've always got along all right.

WAITER: Bravo.

FRAU BALICKE: You bastard!

KRAGLER: If you've got a conscience, the birds'll shit on your roof. If you've got patience, you'll end up eaten by vultures. They've got it all fixed.

ANNA *suddenly sets off, falls across the table.* Andy! Help me! Help, Andy!

MARIE: What's the matter? What is it?

KRAGLER *looks at her astounded:* Well?

ANNA: Andy, I don't know, I'm so miserable, Andy. I can't tell you anything, you mustn't ask. *Looks up.* I can't belong to you. God knows it. *Kragler drops his glass.* And I'm asking you to go, Andy. *Silence. In the next room the Man can be heard asking 'What's happening?' The waiter answers him, talking through the door left.*

WAITER: The crocodile-hide suitor from Africa has been waiting for four years and the bride still has her lily in her hand. But the other suitor, a man with buttoned boots,

won't give her up and the bride who still has her lily in her
hand doesn't know which side to go off.

VOICE: Anything else?

WAITER: The revolution in the newspaper district is part of
it all and then the bride has a secret, something the suitor
from Africa who has been waiting for four years doesn't
know about. It's still quite undecided.

VOICE: No decision one way or the other?

WAITER: It's still quite undecided.

BALICKE: Waiter! Who are that low-down crowd? Are we
supposed to sit and drink surrounded by vermin? *To
Kragler:* Have you heard enough now? Are you satisfied?
Shut up! The sun was hot, was it? That's what Africa's
for. That's in the geography books. And you were a hero?
That'll be in the history books. But the cheque book's
empty. Hence the hero will be going back to Africa. Period.
Waiter, show that object out! *The waiter starts to tow away
Kragler, who accompanies him slowly and with reluctance. But
Marie the prostitute walks on his left side.*

BALICKE: Chimpanzees' tea-party! *Shouts after Kragler, because it's too quiet:* Wanted meat, did you? It isn't a meat
auction. Pack your red moon up and sing your monkeys
something. I'm not interested in your palm trees. The
whole of you's come out of a novel. Where do you keep
your birth certificate? *Kragler is off.*

FRAU BALICKE: You'll be better for a good cry. But
what's that? Want to drink yourself senseless with all that
kirsch?

BALICKE: What sort of a face is that, anyway? Paper-white!

FRAU BALICKE: No, just look at the child. What are you
thinking of? You ought to lay off now.

*Anna sits behind the table, motionless, almost up against the cur-
tains, ill-naturedly, with a glass in front of her.*

MURK *goes up to her, sniffs her glass:* Pepper! Hell's bells! *She
takes it contemptuously away from him.* Oh really! – What the
hell are you up to with that pepper? You'll be wanting
a hot douche next, will you? Then have to be fixed up

manually, I suppose? Hell's bitches! *Spits and flings the glass to the floor.*

Anna smiles.

Machine-gun fire is heard.

BABUSCH *at the window:* It's starting. The masses are stirring. Spartacus is rising. The slaughter continues.

All stand rigid, listening to the noises outside.

ACT THREE (RIDE OF THE VALKYRIES)

[5] > Street Leading to the Newspaper District [<5]

Red-brick barrack wall from up left to down right. Behind it the city, in dim starlight. Night. Wind.

MARIE: Where are you off to?

KRAGLER *with no cap, collar turned up, hands in his trouser pockets, has entered, whistling:* What kind of a red fig is that?

MARIE: Don't run so.

KRAGLER: Can't you keep up?

MARIE: D'you think someone's after you?

KRAGLER: D'you want to go to bed? Where's your room?

MARIE: But that's no good.

KRAGLER: Yes. *Wants to go on.*

MARIE: It's in my lungs.

KRAGLER: Why tag along like a dog, then?

MARIE: But your[6] . . .

KRAGLER: Pooh, that's been scrubbed! Washed out! Cancelled!

MARIE: What'll you do till morning, then?

KRAGLER: [7]There's knives.

MARIE: Dear Jesus . . .

KRAGLER: Quiet, I don't like it when you scream like that, there's also [8]>schnaps[<8]. What d'you want? I can try laughing if you like. Tell me, did they lay you on the steps before you were confirmed? Scrub that! D'you smoke? *He laughs.* Let's go on.[9]>

MARIE: There's firing down by the newspaper offices.[<9]

KRAGLER: We might be useful. *Exeunt both.*

Wind. Two men in the same direction.

THE ONE: I think we'll do it here.

THE OTHER: Mightn't have a chance down there . . .

They make water.

10>THE ONE: Gunfire.

THE OTHER: Hell! In the Friedrichstrasse!<10

THE ONE: Where you watered the synthetic alcohol.

THE OTHER: That moon alone's enough to drive you crazy.

THE ONE: When you've been selling doctored tobacco.

THE OTHER: All right, I've sold doctored tobacco, but you've stuffed human beings into rat-holes.

THE ONE: That must be a comfort to you.

THE OTHER: I won't be the only one to hang.

11>THE ONE: You know what the Bolsheviks did? Show us your hands. No callouses? Bang bang. *The Other looks at his hands.* Bang bang. You're getting smelly already.<11

THE OTHER: O God.

THE ONE: Fine business if you turn up in your bowler hat.

THE OTHER: You've a bowler too.

THE ONE: Battered, my dear fellow.

THE OTHER: I can batter mine.

THE ONE: That stiff collar of yours is as good as a hangman's noose.

THE OTHER: I'll sweat till it's soft; you've got button boots, though.

THE ONE: Your waistline!

THE OTHER: Your voice!

THE ONE: Your look! Your way of walking! Your manner!

THE OTHER: Yes, they'll hang me for that, but you've a grammar school face.

THE ONE: I've a mangled ear with a bullet through it, my dear sir.

THE OTHER: The devil!

Exeunt both. Wind.

From the left now the entire Ride of the Valkyries: Anna, as if fleeing. Next her, wearing an evening coat but no hat, Manke, the waiter from the Piccadilly Bar, who behaves as if intoxicated. After them comes Babusch, dragging Murk, who is drunk, pale and bloated.

MANKE: Forget it. He's gone. Blown away. He may be swallowed up in the ¹²>newspaper district<¹² already. They're shooting all over the place, all kinds of things are happening at the newspapers, this night of all nights and he might even be shot. *Speaking to Anna as if drunk:* One can run away when they shoot, but one can also choose not to. Anyhow: another hour and no one will be able to find him. He's dissolving like paper in water. He's got the moon in his head. He's running after every drum. Go! Save your beloved that was, no, is.

BABUSCH *flinging himself in Anna's path:* Halt, all you Valkyries! Where are you going? It's cold and there's a wind too and he's landed in some schnaps bar. *Aping the waiter.* He who waited four years. Nobody's going to find him now, though.

MURK: Nobody. Not a soul. *He sits on a stone.*

BABUSCH: And look at that, will you?¹³

MANKE: He's nothing to do with me. Give him a coat. Don't waste time. He who waited four years is now running quicker than those clouds are drifting. He's gone quicker than this wind is gone.

MURK *apathetic:* The punch had colouring matter in it. Just now when everything's set. The linen got together, the rooms rented. Come over here, Bab!

MANKE: What are you standing about like Lot's wife for? This is no Gomorrah. Does drunken misery impress you? Can you find a way round? Is it the linen?¹⁴ Will the clouds hang back for that?

BABUSCH: What business is that of yours? How are the clouds your affair? You're a waiter, aren't you?

MANKE: My affair? The stars run clean off their rails if a man's left unmoved by unfairness. *Seizes his own throat.* It's driving me too. It's got me by the throat too. A man frightened out of his wits is nothing to be petty about.

BABUSCH: What's that? Out of his wits? Where did you see that? I'm telling you: something's going to be bellowing like a bull down at the newspapers before daybreak.

[15>]And that'll be the mob thinking here's a chance to settle old scores.[<15]

MURK *has stood up, whines:* Dragging a man round in this wind! I feel terrible. What are you running away for? What is it? I need you. It's not the linen.

ANNA: I can't.[16]

MURK: I can't stand on my feet.

MANKE: Sit down! You're not the only one. It's infectious. Father gets a stroke. The drunken kangaroo is in tears. But the daughter goes down to the slums. To her lover who has waited four years.[17]

ANNA: I can't do it.

MURK: You've got all the linen. And the furniture's already in the rooms.

MANKE: The linen is folded, but the bride is not coming.

ANNA: My linen has been bought, I laid it in the cupboard piece by piece, but now I need it no longer. The room has been rented and the curtains hang ready and the wallpaper is up. But he is come who has[18] no shoes and only one coat, and the moths are in that.

MANKE: And he is swallowed up by the [19>]newspaper district[<19]. Awaited by the schnaps saloons. The night! The misery! The dregs! Rescue him!

BABUSCH: All this is a drama called The Angel of the Dockland Boozers.

MANKE: Yes, the angel.

MURK: And you want to go down there [20>]to the Friedrichstrasse?[<20] And nothing's going to stop you?

ANNA: Nothing that I know of.

MURK: Nothing?[21] Won't you still be thinking of 'the other thing'?

ANNA: No. I don't want that any more.

MURK: You don't want 'the other thing'?

ANNA: That's the tie.

MURK: And it doesn't bind you?

ANNA: It's broken now.

MURK: Your child means nothing to you?

ANNA: It means nothing.

MURK: Because he is come who has no coat?

ANNA: I didn't recognize him.

MURK: It's no longer him. You didn't recognize him.

ANNA: He stood in the middle like some animal. [22>]And you[<22] beat him like an animal.

MURK: And he howled like an old woman.

ANNA: And he howled like a woman.

MURK: And cleared off and left you sitting there.

ANNA: And went away and left me sitting there.

MURK: Finished, he [23>]is.

ANNA: And he's finished.[<23]

MURK: He has gone away . . .

ANNA: But when he was gone away and he was finished . . .

MURK: Nothing remained. Absolutely nothing.

ANNA: There was a turbulence behind him and a slight wind and it grew very strong and was stronger than anything else and now I am going away and now I am coming and now it's all finished for us, for me and for him. Because where is he gone? Does God know where he is? How big is the world and where is he? *She looks composedly at Manke and says softly:* Go to your bar, I'm grateful to you, and please see that he gets there.[24] But Bab, you come with me! *And hurries off right.*

MURK *plaintively:* Where's she off to?[25>]

BABUSCH: That's the end of the Ride of the Valkyries, my boy.[<25]

MANKE: The lover has already vanished, but his beloved hastens after him on wings of love. The hero has been brought low, but his path to heaven is already prepared.

BABUSCH: But the lover's going to stuff his beloved down a sewer and take the path to hell instead. O you romantic institute, you!

MANKE: She is vanishing already as she hastens [26>]down to the newspaper buildings[<26]. Like a white sail she can be seen still, like an idea, like a final cadence, like an intoxicated swan flying across the waters . . .

BABUSCH: What are we to do with this sodden clod?

MURK: I'm staying here. It's cold. If it gets any colder they'll come back. You know nothing about it. Because you don't know the other thing. Let her run. He won't want two. He left one behind and got two running after him. *Laughs.*

BABUSCH:[27] She's vanishing heavenwards like a final cadence. *Slogs after her.*

[28>]MANKE *calls after him:* Glubb's bar, Chausseestrasse! That whore with him hangs out in Glubb's bar. *Spreads both his arms widely once more:* The revolution is[<28] swallowing them up. Will they find one another?

A Small Schnaps Distillery

Clad in white, Glubb, the proprietor, sings the 'Ballad of the Dead Soldier'[1] to guitar accompaniment. Laar and a sinister drunk man stare at his fingers. A small square man called Bulltrotter is reading the paper. Manke, the waiter, brother of the Manke from the Piccadilly Bar, is drinking with Augusta, a prostitute, and all are smoking.

BULLTROTTER: I want schnaps, not a dead soldier, I want to read the paper and I need schnaps for that or by God I won't understand it.

GLUBB *with a cold glassy voice:* Don't you feel at home?

BULLTROTTER: Yes, but there's a revolution on.

GLUBB: What for? This is my place where the scum feels at home and Lazarus sings.

THE DRUNK MAN: I'm scum, you're Lazarus.[30>]

A WORKER *enters and goes up to the bar:* Evening, Karl.

GLUBB: In a hurry?

THE WORKER: Hausvogteiplatz at eleven.

GLUBB: Plenty of rumours.

THE WORKER: There's been a guards division at the Anhalt station since six. All quiet at the 'Vorwärts' building. We could do with your boy Paul today, Karl.

MANKE: We don't talk about Paul here usually.

THE WORKER *paying:* Today's unusual. *Exit.*

MANKE *to Glubb:* Wasn't it unusual last November? You need a gun in your hand and a sticky feeling at the tips of the fingers.

GLUBB *chilly:* What can I do for you, sir?

BULLTROTTER: Freedom! [<30] *He takes off his coat and collar.*

GLUBB: Drinking in shirtsleeves is against the law.

[1] See p. 391.

BULLTROTTER: Reactionaries.

MANKE: They're practising the [31]>Internationale<[31], in four parts with tremolo[32]. Freedom! Then I suppose a fellow with clean cuffs will be put to scrub the lavatories?

GLUBB: They'll make a mess of the false marble.

AUGUSTA:[33] So people with clean cuffs are not to scrub the lavatories, eh?

BULLTROTTER: You'll be put up against a wall, mate.

AUGUSTA: Then let them with the clean cuffs be so good as to strap up their arseholes.

MANKE: Augusta, you're crude.

AUGUSTA: O you swine, you ought to be ashamed, your bowels should be ripped out, you should be hanged too, and them with the clean cuffs be strung up a lamp-post. 'Can't you cut the price, ducky, now we've lost the war?' You've no business making love if you haven't got the money, and you've no business making war if you don't know how to. Take your feet down when there are ladies present. Why should I smell your stinking feet, you dirty bugger?

GLUBB: His cuffs aren't a bit clean.

THE DRUNK MAN: What's that rumbling?

MANKE: Guns.

THE DRUNK MAN *gives the others a pale grin:* What's that rattling?

Glubb goes to the window, throws it open, they hear guns racing down the street. All at the window.

[34]>BULLTROTTER: That's the regiment they call the Cock-chafers.<[34]

AUGUSTA: Jesus Christ, where are they going?

GLUBB: To the newspaper offices, girl. They're the readers. *He shuts the window.*[35]

AUGUSTA: Jesus Christ, who's coming in?

Kragler swaying in the doorway as if drunk, rocking on the soles of his feet.

[36]>MANKE: Are you laying an egg in that doorway?<[36]

AUGUSTA: Who are you[37]?

KRAGLER *grinning maliciously:* Nobody.

AUGUSTA *drying him:* The sweat's running down his collar.[38] Been running hard, haven't you?[39]

THE DRUNK MAN: Got squitters?

KRAGLER: No, I've not got the squitters.[40>]

MANKE *goes across to him:* Well, what have you been up to, my boy? I know the type.

MARIE *appears behind him:* He hasn't been up to anything. I invited him, Augusta; he hasn't got anywhere to go. He's been in Africa. Sit down.

Kragler continues to stand in the doorway.[<40]

MANKE: Prisoner of war?

MARIE: And posted missing.

AUGUSTA: Missing too?

MARIE: And a prisoner of war.[41>] And in the meantime they pinched his fiancée.

AUGUSTA: Come to Mummy, then. Have a seat, gunner. *To Glubb:* Five double kirsches, Karl.

Glubb pours out five glasses, which Manke puts on a small table.

GLUBB: Last week they pinched my bicycle.

Kragler goes to the table.[<41]

AUGUSTA: Tell us about Africa.[42>]

Kragler drinks without answering.

BULLTROTTER: Cough it up. The landlord's a red.

GLUBB: What did you say I was?

BULLTROTTER: A red.

MANKE: Mind yourself, sir; there's nothing red about this place, if you don't mind.

BULLTROTTER: All right. Not red, then.

AUGUSTA: And what did you do out there?

KRAGLER: Shot wogs in the belly. Made roads. – Is it your lungs?

AUGUSTA: How long for?

KRAGLER *keeps addressing Marie:* Twenty-seven.

MARIE: Months.

AUGUSTA: And before that?

KRAGLER: Before that? I lay in a hole full of mud.

BULLTROTTER: And what were you doing there?

KRAGLER: Stinking.

GLUBB: Yes, you could lie around as much as you wanted.

BULLTROTTER: What were the tarts like in Africa?

Kragler is silent.

AUGUSTA: Don't be crude.

BULLTROTTER: And when you got back she wasn't at home, eh? I suppose you thought she'd go to the barracks every morning and wait around for you among the dogs?

KRAGLER *to Marie:* Shall I hit him?

GLUBB: No, not yet. Give us a tune on the nickelodeon, that's what you can do.

KRAGLER *stands up swaying, and salutes:* Sir! *He goes and starts up the nickelodeon.*

BULLTROTTER: Mush.

AUGUSTA: It's just that he feels he's a corpse. He's dead but he won't lie down.

GLUBB: Yes, yes. He's been the victim of a slight injustice. He'll get over it.

BULLTROTTER: Here, you're a red, aren't you? Glubb! Weren't they saying something about your nephew?

GLUBB: They were. Not in this house, though.

BULLTROTTER: No, not in this house. At the Siemens works.

GLUBB: For a short while.

BULLTROTTER: For a short while at Siemens's. He worked a lathe. He worked a lathe for a short while. Worked a lathe till last November, didn't he?

THE DRUNK MAN *who has done nothing but laugh so far, sings:*

> My brothers are all dead
> And I was nearly so.
> November I was red
> But January no.

GLUBB: Herr Manke, this gentleman doesn't want to be a nuisance to anybody. See that he isn't.

KRAGLER *has seized Augusta's waist and is dancing round with her:*

'A dog went to the kitchen
To get a bone to chew.
The cook picked up his chopper
And cut that dog in two.'

THE DRUNK MAN *convulsed with laughter:* Worked a lathe for a short while . . .^{< 42}

GLUBB: You're not to smash my glasses, gunner.

MARIE: He's drunk now. It'll be a relief.^{43>}

KRAGLER: A relief, is it? Console yourself, brother Schnapsvat, just say: it's not possible.

AUGUSTA: Drink up, love.

THE DRUNK MAN: Weren't they saying something about a nephew?

KRAGLER: What is a swine in the eyes of the Lord, sister prostitute? He is nothing.

THE DRUNK MAN: Not in this house.

KRAGLER: And why? Can we do away with the army or God? Can you do away with torture, Red, with the torments the devil has learnt from the human race? No, you can't do away with them, but you can serve schnaps.^{< 43} So drink up and shut the door and don't let the wind in, which is frozen too, but put wood between.⁴⁴

BULLTROTTER: The landlord says you're the victim of a slight injustice; you'll get over it, he says.

^{45>}KRAGLER: Will I? Did you say injustice, brother Red? What sort of a word is that? Injustice! A whole lot of little words like that they keep inventing, and blowing in the air, and then they can put their feet up and one gets over it. And big brother clouts his little brother on the jaw, and the cream of society takes the cream off the milk, and everyone gets over it nicely.

THE DRUNK MAN: Over that nephew. The one they say nothing about in this house.

KRAGLER:

'The other dogs came running
To dig that dog a grave
And set him this inscription
Upon the stone above:

A dog went to the kitchen . . .'

Therefore make yourselves at home on our planet, it's cold here and rather dark, Red; the world's too old for the millennium and heaven has been let, my friends.

MARIE: What are we to do, then? He says he wants to <45 go to the newspaper offices. There they are, but what's happening there?

KRAGLER: A cab driving to the Piccadilly Bar.

AUGUSTA: Is she inside?

KRAGLER: With her inside. 46> My pulse is quite normal: feel. *Holds out his hand, while drinking with the other.*

MARIE: He's called Andy.

KRAGLER: Andy. Yes, I was called Andy. *He continues absent-mindedly to feel his pulse.* <46

LAAR: They were mainly fir trees, little fir trees . . .

GLUBB: The stone's starting to talk.[47]

BULLTROTTER: And you sold, you 48> idiot?

LAAR: Me?

BULLTROTTER: Oh, the bank? Interesting, Glubb, but not in this house.

GLUBB: Are you feeling offended? Well, control yourselves then. All right, then prepare to be controlled. <48 Keep calm when they pull the skin off you, gunner, or it may split; it's the only one you've got. 49> *Still busy with glasses:* Yes, you're a bit offended; <49 you've been killed off by guns and sabres, shat on a bit, and spat on a bit. 50> Well, what about it?

BULLTROTTER *referring to the glasses:* Aren't they clean yet?

THE DRUNK MAN: Wash me, Lord, that I may become white! Wash me that I may become white as snow! *Sings:*

My brothers all are dead, yes dead
And I was very nearly so.
November I was red, ah red
But January no . . .

GLUBB: That'll do.

AUGUSTA: You cowards!

NEWSPAPER WOMAN *enters:*^{< 50} Spartacus threatens press offices! Red Rosa speaks at Zoo!⁵¹ Mob rule for how long? Where are the troops? Ten pfennigs, soldier? Where are the troops: ten pfennigs. *> Exit, as there are no customers.*

AUGUSTA: And Paul not there.<

KRAGLER: That whistling again?^{52>}

GLUBB *closes his cupboard, dries his hands:* We're closing.

MANKE: Let's go, Augusta. He's saying nothing against you, but let's go. *To Bulltrotter:* Anything the matter, sir? Two marks sixty.

BULLTROTTER:^{< 52} I was at Jutland; that was no picnic either.

^{53>}THE DRUNK MAN *with his arm round Marie:*

The saintly slattern disappears
Swimming with him through floods of tears.^{54>}

KRAGLER: Down to the papers, everyone!

'A dog went to the kitchen
To get a bone to chew.
The cook picked up his chopper
And cut that dog in two.'^{< 54}

LAAR *staggers to the nickelodeon, pulls the drum away and starts a roll, swaying after the others.*

Wooden Bridge

Shouting, big red moon.

BABUSCH:[55] It's time for you to go home.

ANNA: I can't go back there.[56] What's the use, I waited four years with a photo and took another man. I was frightened at night.

BABUSCH: I've run out of cigars. Aren't you ever going home?[57] They're flinging torn-up papers in the puddles, screaming at machine-guns, shooting in each other's ears, imagining they're building a new world. Here's another group coming now.

ANNA: There he is!

As the group approaches there is a great disturbance in the street. Shooting breaks out in many directions.

ANNA:[58] I'm going to tell him.

BABUSCH: I'll stop you.

ANNA: I'm not an animal. I'll scream!

BABUSCH:[59] And I've run out of cigars.

From between the houses come Glubb, Laar, the drunk man, the two women, the waiter Manke from the Piccadilly Bar, and Andy Kragler.

KRAGLER: I'm hoarse. I've got Africa in the throat. I'm going to hang myself.

GLUBB: Why not hang yourself tomorrow and come with us to the newspaper buildings now?

KRAGLER *stares towards Anna:* Yes.

AUGUSTA: Seen an apparition?

MANKE: Hey, your hair's standing on end.

GLUBB: Is that her?

KRAGLER: What's the matter, then; are you stopping here? I'll have you shot. March, march, double march!

ANNA *goes to meet him:* Andy!

THE DRUNK MAN: Lift your leg, I spy love!

ANNA: Andy, stop a moment, it's me, I wanted to say something. *Silence.* I wanted to remind you of something; stop just a moment, I'm not drunk. *Silence.* [60]You've no cap, either; it's cold. I must say something to you privately.[61]

KRAGLER: Are you drunk?

AUGUSTA: His fiancée comes after him, and his fiancée's boozed.

ANNA: What do you think? *Walks a few steps.* I'm with child. *Augusta laughs shrilly.*
Kragler sways, squints towards the bridge, springs around as if trying out walking.

AUGUSTA: Are you a fish, gasping for air like that?

MANKE: You must think you're asleep.

KRAGLER *hands down his trouser seams:* Sir!

MANKE: She's with child. Having children's her business. Come on!

KRAGLER *stiffly:* Sir! Where to, sir?

MANKE: He's gone off his head.

GLUBB: Usedn't you to be in Africa?

KRAGLER: Morocco, Casablanca, Hut 10.

ANNA: Andy!

KRAGLER *listens:* Listen! My [62>]fiancée,[<62] the whore! She's come, she's there, she's got a bulge in her belly!

GLUBB: She's a bit anaemic, isn't she?

KRAGLER: Sh! It wasn't me, I didn't do it.

ANNA: Andy, there are people around.

KRAGLER: Is your body blown up with air or did you make a whore of yourself? I was away; I couldn't keep an eye on you. I was lying in the filth. Where did you lie while I was lying in the filth?

MARIE: You shouldn't speak like that. What do you know about it?

KRAGLER: And it was you I wanted to see. Otherwise I'd be lying where I belong, would have wind in my skull, dust in my mouth, and know nothing. But I wanted to see you first. I wouldn't settle for less. I ate husks. They were bitter. I crept on all fours from my hole in the mud. That was comic. Swine that I am. *Opens his eyes suddenly.* Have a good look, eh? Did you get free tickets?

He picks up lumps of earth and throws them about him.

AUGUSTA: Hold him down!

ANNA: Throw them, Andy! Throw them! Throw them at me!

MARIE: Get the woman away, he'll stone her to death.

KRAGLER: Go to the devil! You've everything you need! Open your mouths. There isn't anything else.

AUGUSTA: Down with his head! Rub it in the dirt!

The men hold him to the ground.[63]

AUGUSTA: Blow, will you, miss?

GLUBB *to Anna:* Yes, you go home, the early morning air's no good for the ovaries.

BABUSCH *crosses the battlefield to Kragler, and tells him while chewing his mangled cigar:* That'll teach you where the shoe pinches. You're God; you've thundered. As to the woman, she's pregnant, she can't go on sitting on that stone, the nights are chilly, perhaps you'll say something . . .

GLUBB: Yes, perhaps you'll say something.

The men allow Kragler to get up. There is silence, the wind is heard, two men pass by in a hurry.

[64>]THE ONE: They've got the Ullstein building.

THE OTHER: And artillery's getting into position outside the Mosse building.

THE ONE: We're far too few.

THE OTHER: Far more are on the way.

THE ONE: Far too late.

They have passed.[<64]

AUGUSTA: There you have it. Pack it in.

MANKE: Stuff the answer down his gullet, that bourgeois and his tart!

AUGUSTA *tries to drag Kragler along:* Come along to the newspaper buildings, love! You're beginning to wake up.

GLUBB: Let her stay on her stone if she wants. The underground starts at seven.

AUGUSTA: It won't be running today.[65]

THE DRUNK MAN: Forward, forward to alleluia!

Anna has risen to her feet again.

MARIE *looks her over:* White as a sheet.

GLUBB: A bit pale and a bit thin.

BABUSCH: She's on her way out.

GLUBB: It's just the unflattering light. *Looks at the sky.*

AUGUSTA: [66>]Here come the workers from Wedding.[<66]

GLUBB *rubbing his hands:* You came with the guns. Perhaps you belong with them. *Kragler is silent.* You don't say anything, that's sensible. *Walking round.* Your tunic's been slightly shot up, and [67]altogether you're a bit pallid, a bit worn down.[68] But it doesn't much matter. The only slightly displeasing thing is your shoes, they squeak. But you can put grease on them. *He sniffs the air.* [69]Of course, one or two star-spangled skies have gone under since eleven and a number of Redeemers have been gobbled up by the sparrows, but I'm glad you're still there. Just your digestion worries me. All the same you aren't transparent yet, at least one can see you.

KRAGLER: Come over here, Anna.

MANKE: 'Come over here, Anna'.[70]

ANNA: Where is the underground, does anyone know?

AUGUSTA: No underground today. No underground, no elevated, no local services, for the whole of today. Today there will be universal rest, on all tracks today the trains will be stopped, and we shall walk around like civilized people till evening, my dear.

KRAGLER: Come over here to me, Anna.

[71>]GLUBB: Won't you come along for a bit, brother gunner?[<71]

Kragler is silent.

GLUBB: One or two of us would like to have drunk another schnaps or so, but you were against it. One or two would like to have slept in a bed again, but you hadn't

got a bed, [72>] so it was no good planning to go home
either.

Kragler is silent. [<72]

ANNA: Won't you go, Andy? They're waiting for you.

MANKE: Fish your paw out of your pocket, mate, anyhow.[73]

KRAGLER: Fling stones at me, here I am: I can rip the shirt off
my back for you, but bare my throat to the knife, I will not.

THE DRUNK MAN: Heaven, arseholes and little bits of string.

AUGUSTA: And and and the newspapers?[74]

KRAGLER: It's no use. I won't let myself be dragged down to
the newspapers in my shirtsleeves. I'm not a lamb any more.
I don't want to die.[75] *Takes his pipe once more from his trouser
pocket.*[76]

GLUBB: A bit pathetic, isn't it?

KRAGLER: Look, they'll riddle your chest like a sieve.
[77>] Anna! What the devil are you looking at me like that
for? Have I got to defend myself to you too? *To Glubb:*
They shot your nephew, but I've got my wife back. Anna,
come.

GLUBB: It looks as though we'd better go on without him. [<77]

AUGUSTA: Then was all that lies, Africa and so on?

KRAGLER: No, it was true. Anna!

MANKE: The gentleman was bellowing like a stockbroker
and now he wants his bed.

KRAGLER: Now I've got my wife.

MANKE: Have you got her?

KRAGLER: Here, Anna. She is not untarnished, nor is she
innocent; have you been an honest woman or have you got
a brat in your body?

ANNA: A brat, yes, I've got one.

KRAGLER: You've got one.

ANNA: Here he is, inside here, the pepper didn't do any good
and my figure has gone for ever.

KRAGLER: Yes, that's her.

MANKE: And us? Soaked to the heart in schnaps and filled to
the navel with talk, and with knives in our paws, and who
did they come from?

KRAGLER: They came from me. *To Anna:* Yes, that's the sort you are.

ANNA: Yes, that's the sort I am.

GLUBB: You didn't yell 'To the newspaper buildings!' I suppose?

KRAGLER: Yes, I did that. *To Anna:* Walk over here.

MANKE: Yes, you did that, it'll be the end of you, mate, you yelled 'To the newspaper buildings!' all right.

KRAGLER: And I'm going home. *To Anna:* 78>Get moving<78.

AUGUSTA: You swine.

ANNA: Let me alone. I pretended to Father and Mother, and I lay in bed with a bachelor.

AUGUSTA: Swine too.

KRAGLER: What's the matter?

ANNA: I bought the curtains with him. And I slept with him in the bed.

KRAGLER: Stop it!

MANKE: Look, mate, I shall hang myself if you change your mind.

A distant shouting off.

AUGUSTA: 79>They're attacking the Mosse building.<79

ANNA: And despite the photo I forgot everything about you.

KRAGLER: Stop it.

ANNA: Forgot! Forgot!

KRAGLER: 80>And I don't give a damn.<80 Am I to fetch you with my knife?

ANNA: Yes, fetch me. Yes, with the knife.

MANKE: 81Into the water with that lump of rotten flesh!

They fling themselves on Anna.

AUGUSTA: Yes, let's get rid of his tart!

MANKE: Get a hand on her neck!

AUGUSTA: Under water, that profiteer's tart!

ANNA: Andy!

KRAGLER: Hands off!

No sound but panting.

In the distance dull gunfire is heard irregularly.

MANKE: What's that?

AUGUSTA: Artillery.

MANKE: Guns.

AUGUSTA: God have mercy now on all of them down there. They're bursting open like fishes.

KRAGLER: Anna!

Augusta runs upstage, bent double.

BULLTROTTER *appears on the bridge upstage:* For God's sake, where are you all?

GLUBB: He's going to the lavatory.

MANKE: Louse. *Making his way off.*

KRAGLER: I'm going home now, dear man.

GLUBB *has reached the bridge:* Yes, [82]you've got your balls intact.

KRAGLER *to Anna:* It's whistling again, hold on to me, Anna.

ANNA: I'll make myself very thin.

GLUBB: You'll hang yourself all the same, tomorrow morning in the lavatory.

Augusta and the others have already gone.

KRAGLER: You're heading for the wall, man.

GLUBB: Yes, my boy, the morning will see quite a lot of things.[83] Some people will manage to get away safely, of course. *He disappears.*

KRAGLER: They almost drowned with weeping over me and I simply washed my shirt in their tears. Is my flesh to rot in the gutter so that their idea should get into heaven? Are they drunk?

ANNA: Andy! None of it matters.

KRAGLER *doesn't look her in the eyes, wanders around, grips himself by the throat:* I'm fed up to here. *He laughs irritably.* It's just play-acting. Boards and a paper moon and the butchery off-stage, which is the only real part of it. *He walks round again, his arms dangling, and in this way he fishes up the drum from the schnaps bar.* They've left their drum. *He bangs on it.* [84>Half a Spartacist<84] or The Power of Love; Bloodbath round the Newspaper Offices, or [85>Everybody is Top Man in His Own Skin.<85] *Looks up, blinks.* To do or to die. *He drums.*

The bagpipes play, the poor people die around the newspaper buildings, the houses fall on top of them, the dawn breaks, they lie like drowned kittens in the roadway, I am a swine and the swine's going home. *He draws breath.* I'll put on a clean shirt, my skin's intact, my jacket I'll take off, my boots I'll put grease on. *Laughs unpleasantly.* The shouting'll all be over tomorrow morning, but tomorrow morning I shall lie in bed and reproduce myself so I don't die out. *Drum.* Stop that romantic staring! You racketeers! *Drum.* You bloodsuckers! *Laughing full-throatedly, almost choking.* You cowardly cannibals, you! *His laughter sticks in his throat, he cannot continue, he staggers around, throws the drum at the moon, which was a lantern, and drum and moon together fall into the river, which is without water.*[86] Very drunken and infantile. Now comes bed, the great, white, wide bed, come!

ANNA: Oh, Andy!

KRAGLER *leads her off:* Are you warm?

ANNA: But you've got no coat on. *She helps him on with it.*

KRAGLER: [87]>It's cold.<[87] *He wraps her scarf round her neck.* Come now.

[88]*The two walk side by side, without touching one another, Anna slightly behind him. In the air, high up, a long way off, a white, wild screaming: it comes from the newspaper buildings.*

KRAGLER *stops, listens, puts his arm round Anna:* It's now four years.

As the screaming continues they walk away.

Notes and Variants

BALLAD OF THE DEAD SOLDIER
(*Sung by Glubb at the beginning of Act 4*)

And when the war reached its fifth spring
with no hint of a pause for breath
the soldier did the obvious thing
and died a hero's death.

The war, it appeared, was far from done.
The Kaiser said, 'It's a crime.
To think my soldier's dead and gone
before the proper time.'

The summer spread over the makeshift graves.
The soldier lay ignored
until one night there came an offi-
cial army medical board.

The board went out to the cemetery
with consecrated spade
and dug up what was left of him
and put him on parade.

The doctors sorted out what they'd found
and kept what they thought would serve
and made their report: 'He's physically sound.
He's simply lost his nerve.'

Straightway they took the soldier off.
The night was soft and warm.
You could tip your helmet back and see
the stars they see at home.

They filled him up with a fiery schnaps
to bring him back to life
then shoved two nurses into his arms
and his half-naked wife.

The soldier was stinking with decay
so a priest goes on before
to give him incense on his way
that he may stink no more.

In front the band with oom-pah-pah
intones a rousing march.
The soldier does like the handbook says
and flicks his legs from his arse.

Their arms about him, keeping pace
two kind first-aid men go
in case he falls in the shit on his face
for that would never do.

They paint his shroud with the black-white-red
of the old imperial flag
with so much colour it covers up
that bloody spattered rag.

Up front a gent in a morning suit
and stuffed-out shirt marched too:
a German determined to do his dut-
y as Germans always do.

So see them now as, oom-pah-pah
along the roads they go
and the soldier goes whirling along with them
like a flake in the driving snow.

The dogs cry out and the horses prance.
The rats squeal on the land.

They're damned if they're going to belong to France:
it's more than flesh can stand.

And when they pass through a village all
the women are moved to tears.
The party salutes; the moon shines full.
The whole lot give three cheers.

With oom-pah-pah and cheerio
and wife and dog and priest
and, among them all, the soldier himself
like some poor drunken beast.

And when they pass through a village perhaps
it happens he disappears
for such a crowd comes to join the chaps
with oompah and three cheers. . . .

In all that dancing, yelling crowd
he disappears from view.
You can only see him from overhead
which only stars can do.

The stars won't always be up there.
The dawn is turning red.
But the soldier goes off to a hero's death
just like the handbook said.

In memory of Christian Grumbeis, infantryman, born on
11 April 1897, died in Holy Week 1918 at Karasin (Southern
Russia). Peace to his ashes! He could take it.

[Appendix to the 1922 edition. Now in the 'Hauspostille' section
of Brecht's collected poems, dated 1918, less the dedicatory note
and under the title 'Legend of the Dead Soldier'.]

NOTE FOR THE STAGE

At Caspar Neher's suggestion this play was performed in Munich with the following scenery. Pasteboard screens some six feet high represented the walls of the rooms, with the big city painted in childish style behind them. Every time Kragler appeared the moon glowed red a few seconds beforehand. Sounds were thinly hinted. In the last act the Marseillaise was performed on a gramophone. The third act can be left out if it fails to work fluently and musically and to liven up the tempo. It is a good idea to put up one or two posters in the auditorium bearing phrases such as 'Stop that romantic staring'.

[GW *Stücke*, p. 70. In all previous editions the words 'At Caspar Neher's suggestion' were absent and a second phrase 'Everybody is top man in his own skin' included at the end.]

NOTE TO THE SCRIPT OF THE BERLIN PRODUCTION

A small stage, consisting of wood and pasteboard. Thin flats, only partly painted. Doors, windows, walls all have a makeshift air. Similarly, although the great revolutionary operation steadily grows in power offstage it makes only a thin, ghostlike effect in the auditorium. The persons nevertheless must be extremely real and the acting naïve. The auditorium contains posters with phrases from the play such as 'Everybody is top man in his own skin' and 'The eye of the Lord maketh the cattle fat' and 'Stop that romantic staring'.

[Unpublished. Brecht Archive typescript no. 2122 and 1569. This production was in December 1922.]

PREFACE TO 'DRUMS IN THE NIGHT'

I

Conversation with George Grosz

What the bourgeoisie hold against proletarians is their bad complexion. I fancy that what made you, George Grosz, an enemy of the bourgeois was their physiognomy. It's fairly common knowledge that war is currently being waged between the proletariat and the bourgeoisie. To judge by the arguments on both sides it isn't a war that depends on divergences of taste; but those arguments are deceptive and unconvincing, and above all, nobody ever pays them the slightest attention. The bourgeoisie commit injustices, but then injustices are committed on all sides. You and I, George Grosz, are against injustice (like everybody else). But we would be less against it if it could be committed by the proletariat. I mean to say: that can't be the injustice that 'forced you to take up your brushes'. And if it were, then you'd be a counter-revolutionary, and I would shoot you and erect you a monument. I don't believe, Grosz, that over-whelming compassion for the exploited or anger against the exploiter one day filled you with an irresistible desire to get something about this down on paper. I think drawing was something you enjoyed, and people's physiognomies so many pretexts for it. I imagine you becoming aware one day of a sudden overwhelming love for a particular type of face as a marvellous opportunity for you to amuse yourself. It was *The Face of the Ruling Class* [*Das Gesicht der herrschenden Klasse*, one of Grosz's early albums]. I'm not underrating your enjoyment of protest, which was what no doubt moved you to expose as swine the very people who saw themselves as the élite of the human race – and necessarily had to be since none but an élite could be permitted such swinish behaviour. In the Protestant sense there wasn't any truth worth revealing in reducing a proletarian type to his basic pattern. Proletarians have no call to be other than they are. In the immense effort it costs them just to keep alive they spontaneously adopted their most genuine basic form. Any kind of frills were out of the question. In appearing better than he really was, that type of bourgeois was doing business, but proletarians don't do business at all. Art nowadays is in the same position as you: the type you adore as subject-matter you are bound to detest as a member of the public. Politically you regard the bourgeoisie as your enemy not because you are a proletarian but because you are an artist. Your political position (which unlike you I treat as secondary, you see,) is a position in relation to the public, not in relation to your subject-matter. I have gone through the same process as you, just as seriously though with nothing like the same success. Let me refer you to a play of mine which greatly displeased those who share your political opinions: the little comedy called *Drums in the Night*.

2

Drums in the Night's success with the bourgeoisie

This play was performed on some fifty bourgeois stages. Its success, which was considerable, simply proved that I had come to the wrong address. I was totally dissatisfied: why, I could not immediately say. I just had an uncomfortable sensation. I had a vague idea that the people who were so wildly anxious to shake my hand were just the lot I would have liked to hit on the head, not in this play perhaps but in general. My condition was like that of a man who has fired a gun at people he dislikes, and finds these same people coming and giving three cheers for him: inadvertently he has been firing off loaves of bread. When I then consulted the papers to find out what had happened I found that the chief element of my success lay in the furious attacks launched by the aesthetically reactionary press. So there were still those who complained of the loaves!

The whole thing was an aesthetic business of which I understood nothing. In any other period I might have been able to understand something about it, but at this particular moment, with New York being built and Moscow being destroyed, and both processes seeming likely to concern the whole world, aesthetics were wholly irrelevant. The bourgeois theatre, equally incapable of performing the oldest plays or the most modern, imagined that its continued existence was merely a question of styles. Like a foundering ship, the sinking theatre concerned itself with the possibly very difficult but basically unimportant question whether it was better to sink to the left or to the right. And the crew criticized the band, which in its confusion kept on playing 'Nearer, my God, to Thee', meaning the God who is on the side of the big battalions. To avoid dreadful misunderstandings I should point out that this image for the decline of the theatre may perhaps be inappropriate, for the reason that the theatre was a lot more expensive than an old steamship and worth a lot less, and that those who went down in her by no means suffered any loss but quite the reverse. Moreover, a brief bout of introspection was enough to convince audience and artists alike that the theatre was bound to go under; and those shrieks of desperation were paid for by the theatres out of what they made by selling advertising space in the programmes.

I have always regarded myself as a man who, given a few drinks and cigars, can equip himself to turn out a literary work such as careful reflection will lead him to think desirable. The only thing is that I'm not sure what will happen if I give my abilities their head. *Drums in the Night* is an admirable instance of the weakness of the human will. I wrote it to make money. But although, amazingly enough, I really did make money I would be deceiving you if I said that my pains had been rewarded with success. A number of people managed to hand me money for them; but I managed to write a political play.

3

The love story

In view of the fact that my choice of subject for the play was decided on speculative and financial grounds, it is perhaps of public interest that I should specifically have decided that a love story was called for. Writing this play was a really serious business undertaking, which was precisely what made me able to understand the needs of the paying public. (The experiences embodied in the play, in other words, were avarice and writing.) I was accordingly quite ready to supply the love story, but what I found interesting about it above all was of course the property aspect. The character of Kragler, who struck me as a typical hero of our time, reduced it to that. He wanted a particular woman, and the only course open to him psychologically if he didn't get her was that of a man who fails to get a house that he used to, or wishes to, possess. The causes of his desire struck me as not worth going into. I didn't in fact make the woman particularly desirable. She commands a certain run-of-the-mill sensuality, which can hardly be termed strong since it gets satisfied without further ado, and indeed without reference to the object or partner. The entire sexual motivation remains makeshift and ordinary. You or I would call it innocuous. It is not that powerful, almost revolutionary call for physical satisfaction which arises when a woman needs somebody to sleep with her and has to put up with whatever man she can get. To Anna Balicke a man is not an article for use but a cheap luxury. In bourgeois society the erotic sphere is exhausted. Literature reflects this by the fact that sex no longer gives rise to associations. In fact, the strongest erotic life nowadays is probably to be found in that primitive literature (which occurs in the form of certain notoriously efficacious words and) which ordinary people wield with naïve virtuosity. Clearly the significance of their refusal to use vulgar words in front of women is that such words can be relied upon to be thoroughly effective.

Today the tragic potentialities of a love relationship consist in the couple's failing to find a room. Unfortunately, it is difficult to find out whether today's conditions also applied yesterday, as one can hardly ask one's father about his sex life. But at least today one can clearly establish the attraction of vulgar words relating to sex and its organs. Enjoyment of dirty words largely depends on their guaranteed obscenity. Indeed, there are times when enjoyment of sex depends on its guaranteed obscenity. This romantic factor comes into play when Miss Balicke lusts after Kragler's obscene ignominiousness. The bourgeoisie will see it as a triumph of the ideal. In my view not even such depressing considerations as these will deprive the love story in question of its charm.

It may also be that real sexual enjoyment is now only to be got from venereal diseases. Here is a dumping-ground for our feelings where there is still some activity going on. One of these venereal diseases is pregnancy. Murk, whose rootlessness is due to the woman's indifference – a very common pestilence that can truly be compared with those in the Bible – goes and infects her with a child. His conduct is moral: in occupying her troubled mind he improves his economic standing. But morality is there to prevent miscalculations. And the woman behaves immorally. She thinks she will get more from that atmosphere of obscene sexuality: from lying with Kragler when in a pregnant condition.

4

1918: The Kraglers' Revolution

When the play proved successful what succeeded was the love story and the use of drums offstage. (At the same time I'm prepared to admit that a certain fresh and personal quality and a fairly unrestrained penchant for putting things in a poetical way counted in my favour.) My interest in the revolution whose job it was to serve as background was about as great as the interest felt in Vesuvius by a man who wants to boil a kettle on it. Moreover, my kettle seemed to me a very large affair compared with the volcano in question. It truly wasn't my fault that the play ended up by giving something like a picture of the first German revolution and, even more, a picture of this particular revolutionary.

This revolution followed after a war which originated in a nervous breakdown on the part of the diplomats and was finished off by the military. The bourgeoisie waged it with particular force. Wars have been waged before now for sillier reasons than the annexation of the coal and iron-ore districts of Briey. That famous dagger which the proletariat thrust into the army's back (the legend of which went on . . . buzzing a long while in people's heads) would, if successful, have struck a region the army had long since abandoned; defeated, it was withdrawing. That was where the Kraglers came in. They made a revolution because their country, which some of them hadn't seen for four years, had changed. The Kraglers were rigidly conservative. Thanks to the sudden disappearance from all government positions of that part of the bourgeoisie which was aware that it was the bourgeoisie, the part which wasn't (i.e. the Social Democrats) was put in the embarrassing situation of having to fill them. These men were revolutionaries in the sense that miners in an insecure pit are mining engineers. The problem for the Kraglers was how to become bourgeois. Most people treated them as revolutionaries, and on the stage indeed I found that Kragler gave a very revolutionary impression. Above all, he gave the impression of being a proletarian. Of course the military had been proletarianized. Their complexion was not what it used to be. Factories had always been like barracks, and now it could be seen that they had similar effects. For a while the true revolutionaries could deprecate the play, since they took Kragler to be a proletarian and had learnt what good heroes such proletarians make. They could also oppose it on the grounds that they took Kragler to be a bourgeois and didn't want a hero like that. For there wasn't any doubt about his being a hero. Today, however, they could no longer deny that it is a thoroughly political play. An object-lesson such as one seldom gets. What they had before them was that disastrous type of Social Democrat, and in his heroic incarnation at that. It was difficult to identify him as a bourgeois, either on the stage or in real life. The revolution had undeniably been lost. This was the type that had made it. What mattered most was to learn how to identify him. He had made it, and here he was. Here, in an ordinary romantic love story with no particular depth to it, was this Social Democrat, this fake proletarian, this catastrophic revolutionary who sabotaged the revolution, who was more bitterly fought by Lenin than the bourgeois proper, and who so evaded even Lenin's grasp that before the Russian revolution it was scarcely possible to identify him to the masses so that they could be warned. This, then, was Kragler, this revolutionary whom sympathy converted back into a property-owner, who wept and nagged and, as soon as he got what he had been lacking, went home. As for the proletarians, they were not shown the play.

[GW *Schriften zum Theater* 3, p. 960 ff.
Written after Brecht's move to Berlin.]

NOTES OF CONVERSATIONS ABOUT 'DRUMS IN THE NIGHT'

BRECHT: Ten years since I wrote it. The whole business pretty strange to me now. What I saw was important. Possibly a lot there that I failed to see. Total impression a wrong one. Kragler = drama of the individual. But impossible to depict the German revolution as drama of the individual. I see him coming back after the war. He finds home devastated, no place for him. One's shown what happened to the fellow. But not shown, e.g. that the fellow is first-rate material; not shown him in any situation where the revolution can make use of him; not shown how the revolution fails to do this. The way Lenin would have seen him: out of reach for four years, but submitted to increasing revolutionary tension. If he would have ratted none the less, then play bad. That isn't what happens, though.

PISCATOR: That would make sense if there'd been nobody capable of showing. But you had Liebknecht, Luxemburg . . . When the troops came back from the war the line was all of a sudden: 'Take part in the Workers' and Soldiers' Councils!' Play needs changes. The man was a prisoner. Doesn't alter the position. Battle for the newspaper offices. Everyone knew the proletarian slogans. Only a half-wit could avoid them. Can Kragler remain so ignorant and apart? Then he's an individual case, not a typical worker. Didn't act as a blackleg either. No feeling either for or against the revolution . . . That's as close as one can get to him. There lies the tragedy, but it didn't originate with Kragler. The tragedy about Kragler . . .

BRECHT: He's not tragic.

PISCATOR: The world around him's supposed to seem tragic. The tragedy is that the German revolution is a failure, that people aren't faced with a challenge.

BRECHT: Tragic or not tragic, from the point of view of the revolution it's wrong that no approach was made to the man.

PISCATOR: Establish the crux. The man turns up as an ex-prisoner. Chance is the decisive factor in the situation. He's always having to circumvent chance incidents.

STERNBERG: The 1918 revolution must be present in the background. I'd say that, now we've got a militant red organization, the German Communist Party, we're too apt to project everything back to the 1918 period, which is something Brecht has instinctively avoided doing. The slogan 'Convert the war into a civil war!' only dates from the beginning of the revolution. This was one thing in Russia, where they already started trying to convert a war into a civil war in 1905, and another in Germany, where social democracy was a force. (New number of *Klassenkampf* today: Ebert wanted to save the monarchy as late as 9 November: the leader of social democracy!) That's how things were in 1918 when the troops came home. So and so many million workers were then in the same sociological situation. They had the same programme as the majority Socialists: let's hope we get in. There must have been a tremendous preponderance of pacifist forces to detach a worker from the revolution.

BRECHT: Needs every possible force to get his girl back.

STERNBERG: The girl's running away isn't an occasion for making a revolution. But suppose you were a German worker who had been slung into the war and badly misused and had heard one side's slogans, then you would have to be a lot more positive in your attitude to the revolution. In the days of the Spartacists there were 8 million workers coming back from the war and 2 per cent who joined in.

PISCATOR: Projecting back is something we do with Shakespeare as well as with Brecht. Seeing things in a present-day light.

BRECHT: But not modernizing a 1918 play.

PISCATOR: You mustn't forget, though, that you're now seeing what you failed to see then. Today's angle on the subject is a new one. Not a question of seeing further; that's not possible. The new viewpoints are different and must be brought into use too. Piscator came back to Berlin at the beginning of January. Factories all striking, workers all parading with enormous signs along Unter den Linden. More workers coming the other way with signs saying 'Liebknecht, Luxemburg', both groups grabbing each other's signs. Fighting, till somebody shoots. All the workers on the streets. Everywhere small parties of people arguing.

BRECHT: Make him just a historian. Kragler was part of the general movement. Hearing different advice from all directions, 'You must save the revolution – You must carry on the revolution – You must pull back, reconstruct – Bourgeois republic's the pattern now – etc.' He is simply raw material. And on the third day? He goes home. He counts how much money he's got in his pocket, and goes home.

PISCATOR: That'd be an exceptionally calculated reaction.

BRECHT: An Ebert man, who really does reckon that private life's more important.

PISCATOR: In that case the line has got to be drawn very clearly. He must connect up with the subject if he's to be dramatic. As it stands, the play is felt poetically. Brecht saw the man splitting the movement rather than the movement itself. Brecht today is looking back at the revolution scientifically; in those days he was a poet.

BRECHT: All the same, Kragler does notice one or two things. He's been told he must go along, he's faced with the choice of going along, he doesn't go along, he has an extremely bad conscience, he feels he's a swine, that it's a cheap drama. It ends with him saying, 'I'm a swine, and the swine's going home.'

STERNBERG: That's the crux. Piscator's right.

BRECHT: He turns against the revolution, rejects it; he's for romanticism. (The Russian revolution classic, the German not.)

PISCATOR: You may say I look at the revolution romantically, but Liebknecht and Luxemburg didn't.

STERNBERG: What he said agrees with Piscator's view. He's a chance instance. Finds the revolution romantic.

BRECHT: Bunk, according to a lot of people.

[. . .]

PISCATOR: What are they sitting at home for? Kragler because he realizes the revolution's bunk; many others because they're disillusioned.

BRECHT: They're still Kragler. All those you saw, Kraglers. The only kind who weren't Kraglers, the genuine revolutionaries around Rosa Luxemburg and Karl Liebknecht, were the chaps with their eyes open, and they weren't typical. Typical were types like Kragler. He was my revolutionary.

STERNBERG: This is where you need [. . .] film to show how they came to be the majority.

BRECHT: And to get their way.

[. . .]

STERNBERG: I can picture Kragler today sitting in the KPD, a proper communist. A simple type. He's no longer typical today. He's once again subject to the law of decreasing wages, no longer views the revolution as bunk. A type who has undergone a change.

BRECHT: In effect: a man sits there, in this year of grace 1928, talking about 1918. Not at all the same conversation as in 1918. (What with all conversation becoming increasingly political.) In those days he thought about nothing but the woman.

PISCATOR: It's still an isolated case of one individual's drama. Observed by somebody who had nothing to do with the movement.

BRECHT: One can't say that. He'd just as much to do as those million others.

STERNBERG: We're taking one man and showing what they were all like in 1918.

[. . .]

PISCATOR: Why does the play have to be performed?

BRECHT: To show why these people went home, why the revolution came to nothing. Historical enlightenment. The stumbling block was a type who really existed.

PISCATOR: In the hope of showing how revolution can lead to something.

[*Schriften zum Theater* 2, p. 272 ff, shortened as indicated. Not in GW. This conversation, dated 18 November 1928, was followed by another six days later.]

ON LOOKING THROUGH MY FIRST PLAYS (i)

Of all my early plays the comedy *Drums in the Night* is the most double-edged. Here was a case where revolting against a contemptible literary convention almost amounted to contempt for a great social revolt. A 'normal' (i.e. conventional), approach to this story about the returning soldier who joins the revolution because his girl has got engaged to somebody else would either have given the girl back to him or have

denied her to him for good; either way it would have left him
taking part in the revolution. In *Drums in the Night* Kragler,
the soldier, gets his girl back, albeit 'damaged', and puts the
revolution behind him. It seems just about the shabbiest possible solution, particularly as there is a faint suspicion of
approval on the part of the author.

Today I realize that my contradictory spirit – I'm suppressing my wish to insert the word 'youthful' as I hope I still have
it at my disposal in full strength – led me close to the limits of
absurdity.

The 'human predicament' drama of those days, with its un-
realistic pseudo-solutions, was uncongenial to the student of
science. It set up a highly improbable and undoubtedly
ineffectual collective of 'good' people who were supposed to
put a final stop to war – that complicated phenomenon whose
roots lie deep in the social fabric – chiefly by moral condemna-
tion. I knew next to nothing definite about the Russian
revolution, but my own modest experience as a medical
orderly in the winter of 1918 was enough to make me think
that a totally new and different permanent force had entered
the arena: the revolutionary proletariat.

It seems that my knowledge was not enough to make me
realize the full seriousness of the proletarian rising in the
winter of 1918–19, only to show me how unseriously my
obstreperous 'hero' took part in it. The initiative in this fight
was taken by the proletarians; he cashed in. They didn't have
to lose property in order to make them rebel; he got restitu-
tion. They were prepared to look after his interests; he
betrayed theirs. They were the tragic figures, he the comic.
All this, I realized on reading the play, had been perfectly
evident to me, but I could not manage to make the audience
see the revolution any differently from my 'hero' Kragler, and
he saw it as something romantic. The technique of alienation
was not yet open to me.

Reading Acts 3, 4, and 5 of *Drums in the Night* I felt such
dissatisfaction that I thought of suppressing the play. The
only thing that stopped me erecting a small funeral pyre was

the feeling that literature is part of history, and that history ought not to be falsified, also a sense that my present opinions and capacities would be of less value without some knowledge of my previous ones – that is, presuming that there has been any improvement. Nor is suppression enough; what's false must be set right.

Admittedly I could not do much. The character of Kragler, the soldier, the petit-bourgeois, I couldn't touch. My comparative approval of his conduct had also to be preserved. Anyway, even the workers always find it easier to understand the petit-bourgeois who defends his own interests (however sordid these may be, and even if he is defending them against the workers) than the man who joins them for romantic reasons or out of a sense of guilt. However, I cautiously reinforced the other side. I gave the publican Glubb a nephew, a young worker who fell as a revolutionary during the November fighting. Though he could only be glimpsed in outline, somewhat filled in, however, thanks to the publican's scruples, this worker provided a kind of counterpart to the soldier Kragler.

The reader or spectator has then to be relied on to change his attitude to the play's hero, unassisted by appropriate alienations, from sympathy to a certain antipathy.

[From 'Bei Durchsicht meiner ersten Stücke' in GW *Schriften zum Theater*, pp. 945-7. Dated March 1954.]

Editorial Note on the Text

The original version of this play was written in the spring of 1919 and entitled *Spartakus*; no script of it has so far been found. The Brecht Archive has only the typescript of the version used for the Deutsches Theater production of December 1922, three months after the Munich première. The earliest known text is that published by Drei-Masken Verlag in Munich in 1922, which was also reissued twice by Propyläen-Verlag (i.e. Ullstein) in Berlin during the second half of the 1920s. Brecht used it for the first volume of his collected *Stücke* in 1953, with the extensive revisions outlined in his own retrospective note. This revised text was printed, with minor amendments, in the *Gesammelte Werke* of 1967 and is the basis of the present translation.

Three main versions are thus accessible: the 1922 publication, the script of December 1922, and the final text of 1953. The first describes the play as a 'Drama', the other two simply as a 'Play'. In the second the prostitute Augusta is for some reason called Carmen, though Augusta remains a nickname. At some earlier point the Bar in Act 4 seems to have been called 'The Red Grape' (or 'Raisin'): hence the nickname given to one of the waiter brothers in the final version. The confusion in the timing of the action (which is said to take place in November, though the Spartacist revolt and the battle for the Berlin newspaper offices actually occurred in January) was not cleared up till 1967, when a note appeared in GW saying, 'The action of the play now takes place in January 1919.' The most serious divergences between the different versions however occur in Acts 3, 4, and 5, and they represent a seemingly permanent dissatisfaction on Brecht's part with the second half of the play.

This is already on record in his diaries of 1920, even before our earliest version. 'I have rewritten the beginning of Act 3 of *Drums*,' he noted on 3 August, 'and the second (optional) ending to Act 4. . . . I've done four versions of Act 4 and three of Act 5. I've now got two endings, one comic, one tragic.' A little later he is 'dictating *Drums in the Night*. The third act is in the main good; the fourth a bastard, an abortion. . . .' Twenty-five diary pages later he is still at it:

nagging away at *Drums in the Night*. I'm drilling rock, and the drills are breaking. It's terribly hard to make this fourth act follow grandly and simply after the first three, at the same time carrying on the external tension of the third, which works pretty well, and bringing the internal transformation (in 15 minutes) forcefully home. What's more, the play's strong, healthy, un-tragic ending, which it had from the outset and for the sake of which it was written, is the only possible ending; anything else is too easy a way out, a weakly synthetic concession to romantic-ism. Here is a man apparently at an emotional climax, making a complete volteface; he tosses all pathos aside, tells his followers and admirers to stuff it, then goes home with the woman for whose sake he got involved in this extremely dangerous mess. Bed as final curtain. To hell with ideas, to hell with duty!

The contrast between this view of the play and the author's ver-dicts of 1928 and 1954 needs no stressing. Moreover, even by 1922 he had become less certain of the effectiveness of the third act, which seems to have gone badly at the première.

The detailed notes that follow show what passages Brecht cut or changed when he reviewed the 1922 text in the early 1950s. One or two minor amendments apart, the whole of the 1922 edition can be reconstructed from it. The script used by the Deutsches Theater is different yet again, particularly where Acts 4 and 5 are concerned. This would be too complicated to analyse in full, but an account of the more substantial changes follows the extracts from the 1922 edition. It will be found to shed light on one or two obscurities, notably the characters of Glubb and Laar.

VARIANT MATERIAL FROM THE 1922 PUBLISHED TEXT

The figures correspond to the annotations marked in the play. A figure in the play shows where a passage or phrase has been *cut* from the 1922 text. Figures with small arrows show the beginning and end of a passage or phrase which Brecht *rewrote* in the 1950s. In each case the original is given below. There were also a very few entirely new *additions*, which are marked by arrows without figures.

Where the 1922 text ends with a different punctuation mark from that shown in the play the next word should be correspond-ingly amended to start with a capital or lower-case letter, which-ever is required.

A few very minor amendments have been overlooked for the sake of simplicity.

ACT 1
1 It looks as if the revolutionaries are confining their action to the suburbs.

ACT 2
2 *Then an ever-louder sound of stamping feet outside. Shouting. Whistling. Singing. Drumming. The stamping and shouting are prolonged.*
3 and whistling into the cafés.
4 And got drums out in the street?

ACT 3
5 Street Leading to the Slums
6 wife . . .
7 Oh god, there's sleep. There's schnaps. There's tobacco.
8 tobacco
9 down.
   MARIE: They'll be swimming in schnaps down there tonight.
10 THE ONE: They're drumming pretty hard.
   THE OTHER: Hell! In our district!
11 THE ONE: Feeling dizzy?
   THE OTHER: Haven't you got a slow puncture?
   THE ONE: You're getting smelly already.
12 slums
13 Now it's drunk, but once it had buttoned boots and could do what it wanted with a tart on the dance-floor. Still, it's cold now, I'd say, and has no very clear idea what to do. And shouldn't be left lying about.
14 Is it that sack of booze?
15 and that will be him who is frightened out of his wits. I've known him since he was a boy.
   MANKE: To the dogs and to Glubb's schnaps parlour, that's where he'll go. If he's lucky he'll be put up against a wall.
   BABUSCH: He'll choose the schnaps parlour. Or else he'll whistle them all up and when you hear a din towards dawn at the newspapers and there's something drumming in the night: there he goes!
16 MURK: Don't you see me?
   ANNA: Yes.

17 MURK *sobering up:* The linen has been bought and the flat is rented. And where do you want to go?

MANKE: Hear the rabble singing? Where does she want to go? We say: to the little filthy houses, that's where. You know, where one slithers on all the sick on the staircase. To the tumbledown black attics the wind whistles through.

ANNA: That's where I want to go.

MANKE: We're not beaten. The old beds with the rain coming in on them, and how's anyone to keep warm, the wind whistles through. Perhaps it's worse there. You go there! One disappears there. Those are the houses they are drumming in now. Stuffed full of sacks like this one, with no shirt on, and everything takes twenty or thirty years, the last years on this earth, they've never counted and yet your soul feels more at home there than anywhere else.

MURK: Father and Mother are fixing the wedding.

18 waited four years.

MURK: Who has no clean shirt on his body . . .

MANKE: And his skin is like a crocodile-hide!

MURK: Whom you failed to recognize, the way he looked.

MANKE: But the lily was still in her hand when he came.

ANNA: He is come who has

19 slums.

20 To the slums, the darkness, the nothingness?

ANNA: Yes. Into nothingness.

MURK: Nothing but a drunk man's dreams. Nothing but a woman's magazine story. Nothing but a snow of yesteryear.

ANNA: Nothing else . . .

MANKE: That's it: nothing else! She knows now: it's for nothing!

MURK:

21 What about the 'lily'? What about when no breath of wind gets to you and you're frightened out of your wits?

22 MURK: We packed him off. Bag and baggage.

ANNA: And they

23 was, packed off good and proper.

ANNA: And he was finished.

24 He's drunk.

25 Into the wind and I'm so drunk. Can't see my own hands, and she leaves me!

BABUSCH: Now I begin to get it, man. So that's the fish we're frying. That's the end of the Ride of the Valkyries now, my boy. The whole fishy ghost story's starting to turn horribly serious.

26 to the slums.

27 Take it home, do something for your immortal soul.

28 MANKE *drags Murk to his feet, spreads both his arms widely once more, says grandly:* The slums are

ACT 4

29 THE SCHNAPS DANCE

30 BABUSCH *at the window:* Has a man in artillery uniform been here?

GLUBB *pouring schnaps:* No, not here.

BABUSCH *over his shoulder:* He hasn't been here.

GLUBB: Is one supposed to be coming?

Babusch shrugs his shoulders.

GLUBB: Shall I tell him anything?

BABUSCH *looks at Anna, who shakes her head:* No, we'll come back.

Exeunt both.

MANKE: When they grab something it's schnaps, when they share something it's a bed, and when they produce something it's babies. My god, my god. When they had some schnaps in them, dear man, with those pale faces and trembling knees – *he imitates it* – and their nose in the air where it was raining, raining bullets, dear man. And a gun in the hand and a sticky feeling at the tips of the fingers, my boy!

BULLTROTTER: Freedom! Space! Air!

31 Marseillaise

32 , you bourgeois!

BULLTROTTER *throws a newspaper at him:* Where there's a horse there's horseshit. *They throw papers at one another.* Freedom!

MANKE:

33 So that's the sort you are?

34 BULLTROTTER: Riots! Strike! Revolution!

35 BULLTROTTER: But what's that wind?

36 BULLTROTTER: That's fine. He's got an artillery tunic on.

MANKE: A funny sort of casing. Are you laying an egg, then?

37 , turning up with the guns like that?

38 MANKE *goes across to him:* Well, what have you been up to, my boy? I know the type. A row in a bar, eh?

(AUGUSTA *continues:*)

39 MARIE: They took away his beloved he had waited four years
for. They drove to the Piccadilly Bar; he trotted the whole
way to the Piccadilly Bar behind the cab.

THE DRUNK MAN: Like a calf? What a story.

AUGUSTA: A love story?

KRAGLER: None that I know.

BULLTROTTER: Where do you belong? Belong to him?

MARIE: I just ran along with him.

MANKE: What are you running like a calf for?

40 THE DRUNK MAN: Is there a story?

BULLTROTTER: What do you mean, story?

THE DRUNK MAN: Or is it a gospel, perhaps? Give him some
schnaps, let him smoke and then he can tell it. *The door is
shut. Kragler stands against the wall. The others smoke and stare at
his mouth. Glubb wipes glasses.*

THE DRUNK MAN: Keep that door shut. It's only the
wind, brother, but there's wood between. There's wood
between.

KRAGLER *boasting, with sour humour:* I was in Africa ... The
sun's hot there. We shot up wogs, boy, and ... so on. We
were making roads too. We'd gone down there in cattle
trucks.

41 KRAGLER: Ah, Africa. *Silence.* The sun shrivelled your head up
like a dried fig, our brains were like figs, we shot up the
wogs, always in the belly, and worked on the roads and I'd
got a fly in my head, my friends, and no brains left and they
hit me on the head a lot.

BULLTROTTER: That's a true-life story. Well told. Drink up.
What came before that?

KRAGLER: Before that? I lay in a hole full of mud. Like a
corpse in polluted water. We pumped water out. We stared
at the time. It never moved. Then we stared at the sky, a
patch like an umbrella, dark as a puddle always, but anyway
we had the dropsy because the trench was always full. *He
drinks.*

42 AUGUSTA: About Africa! About Africa!

KRAGLER: Well, it never moved, nothing for us to do but
stink. We defended our homes, our native soil and the other
thing, and I defended the lot, the sky and the earth and the
water and – the lot.

MARIE: Andy! They call him Andy.

KRAGLER: Andy! They call me Andy. They used to call me

Andy. Thick green trees in the air, that's something I've seen. But not those four years.

GLUBB: You didn't see them, what of it?

KRAGLER: I defended and now and again somebody fell and I'd got a fly in my head, a fly, and that was my wife, only she wasn't that yet, she was innocent *drinks* and then came Africa.

BULLTROTTER *smiling broadly:* And the tarts down there, what were the tarts like?

KRAGLER: It was like an island. No letters, and chilly nights. *Opening his eyes.* All you people need do is chase cats off a wall! *Drinks.*

MARIE: How long did it last, how long?

KRAGLER: Three years. Three years, that's more than a thousand days. They held us under water, you see, like kittens in a bucket, they don't want to die. *Counting on his fingers.* I could have died the second day, or the tenth, or in twenty days, or in forty days . . . But there was Anna, standing dawn after dawn behind the barracks, among the dogs.

THE DRUNK MAN: Didn't you desert?

KRAGLER *calmer:* The third time I deserted it went well, and I sang when it became too tough, and it went well and there I was. *He sits down, speaks more and more slowly and laboriously, drinks a lot; now he makes a break and says quite calmly:* You mustn't think I was sort of mean and imagined she went to the barracks in the morning and that was all she did. I'd worked out a plan how she was to get accustomed to me once more, because I'd become a ghost. That's a fact. *He drinks. Sound of wind. The drunk man groans with the suspense.*

KRAGLER *calmly:* She wasn't at home when I came.

GLUBB: No, that she wasn't. Truly not.

BULLTROTTER: Well, then?

THE DRUNK MAN: Had she gone? Where was she?

KRAGLER: The schnaps was drunk and the wogs were dead and the umbrella had been rolled up and the fly, the fly had flown off. *Stares ahead.* I defended him. He sent schnaps for the cattle and he sent the umbrella, and he let the fly live so we shouldn't be bored. *Points with his finger as if he could see him.* And now he's going round in the sun, the other fellow. And now he's lying in bed, and you take off your hat when he arrives and he takes the skin off your back and my wife's lying in his bed.

BULLTROTTER *with the paper:* Somebody stole her, eh?

GLUBB: They stole my bicycle.

MANKE *passes his hand across his throat:* I'll say you're patient, mate!

AUGUSTA: Didn't you strangle her like a cat?

MARIE: They went off with her. He just trotted along after.

KRAGLER *drinks:* So I went quite cold when I heard that, and my mind was a blank. And even now my pulse is normal when I think about it; feel for yourselves. *Stretches his hand out, drinks with the other one.* I looked for her and she knew me too, even though my face was once like milk and blood and she said something to me. Give me another glass.

THE DRUNK MAN: Go on. What did she say?

KRAGLER: Yes, she said. *He drinks.* It's all over. *Silence. He is still absent-mindedly feeling his pulse.*

GLUBB: Oh, you'll forget in time.

THE DRUNK MAN: What did you do then?

KRAGLER: Booze away, I'm going. Keep it up, I'm getting out. Jig and drink and drop dead at the right moment. *He is getting noisy.* Me for instance, Africa's in my blood, a nasty malady. A fly in my head, a horsefly, dance up, give me schnaps, they don't know the half of it. Let's have a tune, they're going to know.

MANKE: It's bad, what you've been through. Drink all you like, mate.

BULLTROTTER: Booze yourself silly. He's got a feeling like a corpse, he'll live longer than himself. Last week we had a story from Merseburg . . .

THE DRUNKEN MAN: Is she still alive? *He has started the nickelodeon.* Not possible.

KRAGLER *hums the tune, seizes Augusta, jogs round with her:* March, march, double march!

43 KRAGLER *who is being given schnaps by Augusta upstage:* Is it a relief? Is he paper, isn't he made of flesh? Console yourself, brother, just say: Not possible. Can you hear, brother Schnaps-vat, can you hear the wind? Hop, sister prostitute! Hop, brother Red! I say unto you, you mustn't wait. What is a swine before the Lord? Nothing. Drink yourselves silly, nothing to do with the swine, then you won't notice.

GLUBB: What are you shouting like that for?

KRAGLER: Who's paying here? Who's responsible for the music here? There's always music, isn't there? I've got the fly! I just need schnaps and it'll drown itself. Can we do away with the army or God? Can we do away with suffering and the torments the devil has learnt from the human race? No, we can't do away with them, but we can drink. You can drink schnaps and sleep even on paving-stones. They that sleep, please note, shall find everything of service to them; that's in the catechism, it must be true.

44 Don't let in the ghosts. They are frozen.

45 Did you say injustice, brother Red? What sort of word is that? Injustice! Make yourselves at home on our planet, it's cold here and rather dark, Red, and no time for injustice, the world's too old for the millennium and schnaps is cheaper and heaven has been let, my friends. *Goes upstage humming, puts money in the nickelodeon, which still plays quick short pieces only.*

BULLTROTTER *has been drinking quietly:* What's one to say to that? Cuffs! Cuffs!

MANKE *gets up:* But your wife's looking for you, man.

KRAGLER *dancing on his own:* Trot! Trot! Double march! *Hums.* A dog went to the kitchen to find a bone to chew.

MANKE *smoking:* He's dancing around with his horsefly now.

AUGUSTA: Do you like that tobacco?

GLUBB: Look here, all you may do is drink schnaps.

MANKE: We're smoking as well.

THE DRUNK MAN: You're the revolutionary all right. We know you and your speeches. They poured your schnaps down the lavatory, you were selling schnaps.

GLUBB *still busy with the glasses, coldly:* I'd more under the floor-boards. And it's not because the schnaps went but because of the human hands pouring it down the lavatory.

KRAGLER *blinking and as if he were waking up:* Anna! Anna!

BULLTROTTER *crows:* Cuffs! You ought to have pinched some cuffs, mate.

GLUBB: I was standing in the yard, it was night-time. It was just raining, I looked around, then I suppose it struck me. And now I'm for drinking and I sing.

KRAGLER:

The cook picked up his chopper
And cut that dog in two.

MARIE: What can we do? We're nobodies. A lot of them say:

46 MANKE: Your wife's certainly looking for you, man.

THE DRUNK MAN *has climbed up on the table and is looking out into the night at the city:* Drink, will you?

47 LAAR: There was a fellow who just happened to have some money on him, see.

48 beast?

Laar goes off at the back.

GLUBB *to Kragler, who is much calmer:* Just drink! There are a few people drumming outside and now they've even begun to shoot. One can hear it quite clearly. If one's prepared to shut up for a moment. They're shooting for you. Yes, heaven and hell are making a revolution, man, and you shouldn't even be drinking schnaps. You've suffered a slight injustice. Say yes and stomach it.

49 *Places a glass behind him, calmly:* To the machine-guns with you!

SOME: To the newspaper offices!

GLUBB: Yes, you'll have to publish a paper.

KRAGLER: It's pretty far to the Piccadilly Bar.

MANKE *with a cigar between his teeth, takes his coat off:* If it's too far, there's no need for anyone to let himself be trodden on.

GLUBB *sees the man stand there in shirtsleeves:* Go on, put clean shirts on your decaying skins so nobody will notice them! Are stories just fodder? God alive, a slight injustice! Eat salad and drink kirsch! *Starts up the nickelodeon.* Yes, you people are a bit drowned in brandy, you've been a bit pushed about by rifle-butts,

50 AUGUSTA: You cowards let us starve, then say Amen. A glass of schnaps! *Tumult, consternation.* Look at me. I'm no good and I've not had it good. Just look at me. I'm called Augusta.

GLUBB: And you've got syphilis.

NEWSPAPER WOMAN *in the background:* Papers!

51 State of siege! Revolution!

BULLTROTTER: Give us a paper. That's something for us.

NEWSPAPER WOMAN *shrilly:*

52 *Bends down.* Is it a joke? To the barricades with the ghost! *Stands firmly, draws a deep breath.* A clean end is better than schnaps. It's not a joke. Better disappear than sleep.

BULLTROTTER *leaps on the table:*

53 *Glubb shuts the cupboard full of glasses, dries his hands.*

MANKE: Let's go, Augusta. Do or die.

BULLTROTTER: And how about your distillery, schnaps-seller?

GLUBB: The rats'll take it over.

KRAGLER *on a chair, tinkering with the lamp, a prehistoric survival:* They're whistling again, my friends. On top in the morning or like drowned kittens in the roadway.

THE OTHERS *shout:* On top in the morning, Andy!

KRAGLER *puts out the light:* Or like drowned kittens!

MANKE: Forward, Augusta!

54 KRAGLER *gets down:* I'm a corpse, you're welcome to it. *Angrily.* This way with you, over the top with you, to the newspaper offices with us. *The others follow him.*

THE DRUNK MAN *following behind:* Wash me, Lord, that I may become white! Wash me that I may become white as snow!

ACT 5

55 They stormed the barracks a bit after two.

ANNA: He won't come now.

BABUSCH: Now they're marching to the newspaper offices. Yes,

56 BABUSCH: The last time, somewhere round four, it looked to me as if he'd gone down, he was swimming powerfully but didn't surface.

ANNA:

57 ANNA: How far gone the year is, and how red the moon. Like in one's sleep. I sit here on a stone, and the red moon, and the year's far gone.

BABUSCH: They're drumming again down there.

58 The streets wake up wherever they go. Fever falls through the roofs. The houses become restless.

59 It's fever,

60 Shouldn't you go, though?

61 I've forgotten it now. I suppose it's hopeless.

62 wife

63 GLUBB: She's earth too, my lad; have a look from down there.

64 THE ONE: They've got into the newspaper buildings.

THE OTHER: Artillery's being brought up.

THE ONE: Things will change now.

THE OTHER: They're far too slow, far too few.

THE ONE: Far more are on the way.

THE OTHER: Far too late.

They have passed, but behind them are many marching past to the newspaper buildings.

65 Is his hand still in his trouser pocket?

66 They're marching, they're screaming, they're waving.

67 your lack of hair may be due to the unflattering light.

68 Your fingers are black too: show us.

69 I've known you for just four hours.

70 ANNA: Is it seven?

KRAGLER: Come over to me, Anna.

71 ANNA: So gracious, are you?

GLUBB: Wouldn't you rather have a Scotch?

KRAGLER: Over here to me.

ANNA: Is it because of the catechism?

KRAGLER: Anna.

AUGUSTA: Aren't you a soldier, love?

ANNA: Are you whistling me again?

GLUBB: You must milk a cow while it's still warm.

MANKE: In your army tunic, man?

KRAGLER: My voice is gone with the shouting but my knife's
still there, you!

*Glubb places himself in front of Anna, the tall shadows of the
marchers in the background fall across the buildings, and snatches of
the Marseillaise are borne on the wind.*

GLUBB: Yes, she looks like sicked-up milk, it's not very plea-
sant.

72 and it was the same with smoking a cigar. Which was a pity.

Kragler is silent.

GLUBB: Won't you come along for a bit, brother gunner?

Kragler is silent.

MANKE: What's he staring for in that queer way? Is he laying
another egg?

73 ANNA: You can go, Andy, go on.

AUGUSTA: Now watch him light his pipe again.

ANNA: Go on, go on, I don't want to see you again, you've
got a black face, go away, I'm glad.

74 *Kragler shakes his head.*

Augusta gives a horse-laugh.

GLUBB: The Eternal Feminine is drawing him upwards.

KRAGLER *looking at her:* Come, Anna.

GLUBB: Couldn't you just step into the water and have a bath?

KRAGLER: I'm all cold.

AUGUSTA *upstage:* Only a few left now, they're hurrying,
they're disappearing in no time. Oh, the newspapers, come
on to the newspapers!

GLUBB *to Anna:* Can't *you* get this wild beast down to the newspaper buildings?

75 Everybody is top man in his own skin.

76   GLUBB: So you've no sympathy for these people?

KRAGLER: God help me, stone me, no. What kind of face is that, Anna? Have I got to defend myself to you too? They poured your kirsch down the lavatory, but I've got my woman back. Anna, come.

GLUBB: They could give me six kirsch distilleries, I'd spit in their face because of the kirsch, I'd rip out their bowels because of the kirsch, I'd burn down their houses because of two barrels of kirsch, and smoke as I did it.

KRAGLER: Anna! *To Glubb:* Look! You'll go to the wall and smoke as you do it. I see you against the wall before dawn, can't you see how grey and glassy he looks as he stands against the wall? Can't you smell it in him? What's to become of you all, go home!

Augusta laughs.

GLUBB: Oh, they'll get little wounds in their throat or their chest, all very tidy, they'll get labels with numbers stuck on them when they're stiff, not like drowned kittens, more like victims of a slight injustice.

KRAGLER: Drop it.

77   What'll that do to your chest?

GLUBB *looks coldly at him:* The rats'll take it over.

Across the bridge comes a dolled-up woman.

AUGUSTA: You come from down by the newspaper offices?

THE WOMAN: Yes, down that way.

MANKE: Are they fighting there, how's it going?

THE WOMAN: Nobody knows.

AUGUSTA: Have they taken the newspaper buildings yet, then?

THE WOMAN *raises her arm, there is a distant screaming:* Is that the artilleryman the Friedrichstadt people have been waiting for?

AUGUSTA: Oh, have they been waiting?

THE WOMAN: Yes, there'll be a lot of dead men today. *Exit hurriedly.*

AUGUSTA: You hear, they're going into the attack!

KRAGLER: Anna.

AUGUSTA: Would it be too much bother for the gentleman?

KRAGLER *to Anna:* What are you looking like that for, damn it?

78   Devil!

79   That's the attack going in.

80 And I love you.
81 Now they're being blown open like fishes.
82 the moon's fading out, and
83 The night blows away like black smoke.
84 The Half-Dead Suitor
85 A Man Works his Passage; The Thorn in the Flesh or A Tiger
    at Dawn.
86 *But the man goes to the woman and goes home.*
87 It gets cold, so early in the year.
88 *Like a little flag, the first red appears in the smoky grey dawn sky
    above.*

THE DEUTSCHES THEATER ACTING VERSION

A copy of the Deutsches Theater's typescript is in the Brecht-
Archive in Berlin. It is annotated in pencil (not by Brecht) with a
full cast list, a sketch plan of the stage arrangement for Act 1 and
other production details, and was presumably used for the production of 20 December 1922. This was directed by Otto Falckenberg,
who had also directed the Munich première three months earlier.
Kragler was played by Alexander Granach, Glubb by Heinrich
George, Babusch by Paul Graetz, Anna by Blandine Ebinger.

The introductory note, which differs from that to the 1922
edition, has been given above on p. 60. The Piccadilly Bar
becomes the Grünes Haus (though at one point it has been
changed back in pencil). Augusta becomes Carmen; she is sometimes alluded to as Augusta, and then objects, presumably because
the name is not fancy enough. Kragler on his first entry is described as 'a short, thick-set man', and there is no reference to his
old blue uniform. Otherwise the main changes in the first two acts
are confined to cuts.

There is also a long cut at the start of Act 3, which now begins
with Anna's entry. The stage direction for this begins: *Clouds
racing by. The street runs from upstage left to downstage right. From the
left come . . .* The street leads over a bridge, not along a barrack
wall. The rest of the act is virtually unchanged.

Act 4 starts thus:

*Glubb, a pale desiccated individual with a little red goatee, sings 'The
Ballad of the Dead Soldier' to guitar accompaniment. Two drunks – a
farmer and a sinister man, both drunk – stare at his fingers. Manke
the waiter, a tall fellow, is dancing with Carmen, a blowsy creature. A*

*small square man called Bulltrotter is reading the paper. The drunks
keep on laughing.*

BULLTROTTER: When the landlord's drunk and singing like a
   primadonna, rattling the glasses, then everything's cock-
   eyed. Look at that tart dancing with a shark like that between
   her legs: how the hell is a fellow to digest his paper? You see
   your arse through it. A god-forsaken bar in the back of
   beyond, where the waiter shuffles round the dance-floor
   looking like a shark and the landlord serves him when he
   isn't singing hymns.

BULLTROTTER *putting his feet on the table:* The revolution's on
   the way! Freedom's here!

GLUBB: You're spoiling my fake marbling. *Goes on singing.*

THE DRUNK MAN *to Laar:* Scum and Lazarus. I'm scum, you're
   Lazarus. Heaven, arseholes and bits of string. None of them
   know a bloody thing.

MANKE: When they grab something it's schnaps, when they
   share something it's a bed, and when they produce something
   it's babies. Augusta, come across my knee and pour some
   brandy into me!

BULLTROTTER: That's all talk. Pure grand opera. Where are
   you saying it? In a schnaps bar.

MANKE: Where there's a horse there's horse-shit; that's the
   way, Augusta.

CARMEN: Make up your mind. It's Carmen, or you can dance
   by yourself. Vulgar beast!

MANKE: Ah yes, Augusta, they're practising the Marseillaise, in
   four parts with tremolo. The bourgeois. Well done, landlord.

THE DRUNK MAN: The bourgeois. *Coming forward:* The bourgeois is a necessity, just like the Gents. If it weren't for those
   two institutions public life would be simply immoral.

BULLTROTTER: Change the record. Shut up, landlord! I saw
   the fellows earlier. And they've got a look in their eye, mates,
   or rather landlord, just like before going over the top. You
   know what I mean?

MANKE: I've a notion. When they had some schnaps in them,
   dear man, with those pale faces in the air where it was raining,
   raining bullets, dear man. And guns in their hands and a
   sticky feeling at the tips of the fingers, my boy!

BULLTROTTER: That's how they look, that's how they looked
   just now, just a minute or two ago.

It then continues much as before up to Kragler's entrance, which is slightly different in that the rumble of guns is not heard, and no reference is made to his artillery tunic. His account of his experiences in Africa is also very much as in the 1922 edition (see notes 38–40 above), up to where the nickelodeon plays and he begins dancing with Carmen/Augusta. Then comes an expanded version of Laar's cryptic remarks about the fir trees, (which in both other texts are put later):

GLUBB: Quiet: the farmer's got something to say, the stone is going to speak. Watch out! He's always opening his mouth; now he's made it.

LAAR: But I had land and animals and a wood, simply fir trees, little fir trees.

GLUBB *excitedly watching him :* Listen to the stone speaking, he's speaking now.

LAAR: Nowadays I'm drunk all the time. There was a fellow who just happened to have some money on him, see?
Silence. Kragler sits by the nickelodeon, which has stopped playing. Carmen has her arm round him.

BULLTROTTER: And you sold, you beast?

LAAR: Yes, I did. I didn't want to deliver, and I thought . . . I thought I'd sell instead. It's just a lot of paper, and I handed over my land and my animals, I did, for paper and some schnaps in my gullet. The wife and kids are living like pigs. I live here. We're peaceable folk and we get on; the music plays and the schnaps flows and we say, 'Yes, yes, Amen.' A small schnaps, please.

GLUBB: A small schnaps, please!

MANKE: Can't you get your land back?

GLUBB:
They'll have the whole damn lot –
Wife, land and all you've got.
Let them swallow it . . . etc.

BULLTROTTER: What a world!

CARMEN: It isn't possible.

THE DRUNK MAN: Looks as though it is, mate, so close your eyes. Close your hand, mate.

GLUBB: Isn't it possible? Isn't he flesh and blood? Is he just paper? . . .

Glubb's song 'They'll have the whole damn lot' recurs below. (The songs or jingles in the other two texts are omitted.) Glubb also has more to say about his particular motive for joining the revolutionaries. After The Drunk Man's remark in the 1922 edition (note 45 above), he says:

> Don't insult me. Don't insult anyone, mate. Yes, they poured my schnaps away, just two little barrels; I'd more under the floorboards but it went down the drain because of a regulation on a bit of paper. Mind my words. Since that day I have[n't] slept properly, not because the schnaps went but because of the human hands that poured it down the gutter. Because that's the moment I decided the world was all wrong.

Needless to say there is no hint of this (not even by the Drunk Man) in the 1953 text, where Glubb is relatively silent. Glubb is also given a verse speech, more or less in lieu of his two longer speeches (48 and 49 above). He *climbs on a chair*:

> You who have drowned in schnaps –
> You whose skin is covered in rashes –
> You whom they thrust back with bayonets –
> You whom they gave guns and swords to and turned into murderers –
> You who have always been beaten and spat upon –
> You who were never loved
> Come here and see, your hour is here
> And you shall enter into the kingdom!

Then, as the bullets whistle and the woman selling newspapers appears calling her headlines about the Spartacists, it is he rather than Kragler who leads them all into the street:

> GLUBB: Just keep calm. Come along, all of you, link arms. Join all the others and face up to the soldiers and just let them shoot. And the story will be told wherever there are people who have forgotten their own . . .

These changes in the character and weight of the role persist throughout the next act, and may of course be connected with the powerful talents of Heinrich George, the actor in question. There is none of the disillusioned cynicism of the other versions.

In Act 5 the opening stage direction is again changed:

> *A street corner in the slums. Autumn night. Big red moon. Left, the low pale wall of a house. In the right background a wide wooden bridge, rising towards the rear. Sitting on a stone, left, Anna, who is still wearing her*

*light-coloured dress. Babusch is walking up and down. The wind is
blowing. Distant shots and shouting are heard. Rapid tempo.*

The start of the act is basically as in the other two versions, though
it is somewhat expanded both before and after Kragler's entry.
Then, when Anna has told him she is expecting a child his next
stage direction (*Sways . . . as if trying out walking*) is made to run
on:

> *Then turns and looks round at Anna. Anna sits on the stone and looks
> up at him with as loving a look as she can muster, while he groans and
> shuts his eyes and draws a deep breath. Manke and the drunk man
> approach from the bridge. Glubb squats there, waiting. Behind them
> Marie slowly comes nearer.*

Kragler's attack on Anna with clods of earth is again expanded,
mainly with additional rhetoric that represents no change of sub-
stance. An extra stage direction describes the scene as the men hold
Kragler down and Babusch crosses the battlefield (p. 48):

> *At this point Marie is standing protectively in front of Anna, with her
> arms round her. Glubb has stood up by the bridge. Laar is sitting in the
> roadway, picking dirt out of his hair. Manke is holding Kragler by the
> collar . . .*

Babusch's ensuing speech is likewise expanded, and concludes:

> It isn't a vast idea. The nights are chilly in November.
> You're out to liberate the world, by all means do so, it's an
> excellent thing; but tell the woman that you want no part of
> her. Tell her straight to go home if she can. Don't give us any
> purple passages, no more speeches, it's a small and perfectly
> simple human situation.

The emphasis on the 'idea' is peculiar to this version. The two
Men are cut, with their conversation about how the attack on the
newspaper offices is going. Then from Carmen/Augusta's appeal to
Kragler to come down there (p. 48), to his final refusal with the
speech beginning 'Fling stones at me,' (p. 50) there is an entirely
new section, enlarging on the 'idea'. Thus:

BABUSCH: Say yes or no. Or else you're a coward.
GLUBB: Tell her, Andy. Try to think what you want. Don't tell
her all that quickly. It's as well to say yes or no. Have you got
your idea inside you? It needn't be in the catechism. Tell her.
She'll go away, she's not bad-looking.

THE DRUNK MAN: I'll marry her, let's have her. Because none of them know a bloody thing.

BABUSCH: They don't. Know a thing, I mean. That's to say men don't. Dogs do.

GLUBB: Don't listen to him, Andy. Watch the woman. He's making fun, he has rotten teeth. Watch the woman. Andy! Have you still got your idea? You have to sense it in your throat.

MANKE: What nonsense are you talking? He said, 'To the newspaper buildings'; he's going to the newspaper buildings. Why is he hanging around with his hands in his pockets, trying to get out of it? Come along!

CARMEN *on the bridge:* They're coming! Stop quarrelling. They're coming, lots of them, the streets are black with them, as if they'd gone rotten.

BABUSCH: *He's* got one, Kragler, I'm quite sure. I know the story of his schnaps. But you haven't, though you did have. You've got a gullet full of phrases.

GLUBB: Andy, it's only the devil, but best say yes or no.
The others start concentrating on events offstage, where it seems that masses of people are approaching with drumming and shouts.

BABUSCH: Don't let them make a hero of you, Kragler. If it's what you want it isn't so tragic. Do whatever you really want. Everybody is top man in his own skin.

[There is a blank space in the typescript here.]

MANKE *over his shoulder:* Why doesn't he say something? Has he fallen on his face?

CARMEN: More and more of them are coming, and the whole lot's going to the newspaper offices. Do come along! Isn't it settled?

GLUBB *somewhat hoarsely:* And I'd like to know why you don't say something too. Are you so feeble? It's irritating, your not saying anything. Here we are, charging through the streets like bulls and finding nothing, and you're not with us. God has tossed you your woman, half torn to pieces and with a body full of strange fruit, all you need do is step over her; are you stuck? I tell you, if you're pure a hundred women won't be able to touch you. They're less than an idea, they only mislead you. The swine poured my schnaps in the gutter; it made my head go queer, and no wonder. They can give me a hundred schnaps factories instead of those two small barrels of mine, and I'll still spit in their faces for the schnaps that was

washed away and will never come back. I'll tear out their guts
for that schnaps. I'll burn down their houses for that schnaps
that went down the drain. I'm telling you, Andy, the idea is
what matters.

KRAGLER *angry and obstinate:* No, it isn't.

BABUSCH: Bravo! No, it isn't! When a woman's going to
pieces it isn't the idea that matters.

GLUBB: Well? Do you want to stay back here?

*Offstage crowds are marching by. The wind brings snatches of the
Marseillaise and military band music.*

Kragler is silent.

In all this concluding section of the play Anna now gets given
nothing to say, nor is there any mention of Kragler's knife as in the
1922 edition. His 'fling stones at me' speech ends 'It's a waste of
time, believe me, it's nickelodeon stuff and you're all drunk and
that way you're going to hell.'

GLUBB: Andy, it's not a waste of time. God forbid that you
found it one. There's a thin red flame shooting sharply out of
the human breast and scorching the world.

KRAGLER: What for?

GLUBB: At the innermost heart of the world, racing at the speed
of our planet – a man blown like a leaf, lonely, ice-cold, and
without a home, a man who goes on strike and the world falls
apart.

BABUSCH: Don't be bamboozled; he's got a pigeon's egg in
his head. His talk is all newspaper articles, his ideas are grand
opera. Go to bed. Don't be drunk. Mind the cold wind – it's
November 9th – and go home.

KRAGLER: I was drunk. I'm sober now. It's a waste of
time.

GLUBB: Heaven and hell are full of revolution, and you are
going to bed! Smash your head against the bridge! Jump in
the water and float with the ice; but don't go home!

BABUSCH: You've no coat and it's freezing, Andy. November
nights are cold, and it's nearly morning. Four years is a long
time. Take your woman with you.

GLUBB: Let her lie, let the woman lie. Let her lie where she's
lying on the stones. She's like grass in the wind, she's not
there any more and she doesn't know where she belongs. In
four times four years her face will have faded, and we'll all be
dead by then and wondering where to go next.

BULLTROTTER: The whole lot have gone past, pretty well. We're last, and you're still hanging back.

CARMEN: They're last, and they're still hanging back.

GLUBB: And we're hanging back. He'll never let her lie, the world will roll on, and they'll let the schnaps go down the gutter and nothing'll ever change. O Andy, come with us. We're setting off into the dark, into our most crucial hour. Don't abandon us. What can we do with the schnaps in our heads if there are so few of us? What will the beast do if we're beaten? I've known you for only four hours, yet in that time whole skies full of stars have floated away and kingdoms have surrendered. I've known you for four ages; oh, don't disappoint me.
Silence.
Why do I have to stand here at a street corner in the dark after all those years, so they can shoot me tomorrow? Wrestling with you for your soul, and my hands not strong enough? Look: none of these people are any help to me.

KRAGLER *calmly:* We all know a lot of unfortunates go under, and if it's in our power we give a hand. But I'm nearly done for myself and must fight for dear life. My girl's with child.

GLUBB: Is that all you have to say?

CARMEN: Coward! Coward! He's shaking like a jelly because he heard shots. He isn't coming with us, you bet, he's going to take cover. In her body, which has already got something in it.

KRAGLER *calmly:* Don't you think it takes rather more to go home now and tell the hyenas 'I want no part of it', and say to the sharks as they swim round under the red moon hunting for corpses 'I've got some procreating to do'? More than to run along after you lot yelling something I don't believe in?

THE DRUNK MAN: Look at the old blood-orange! Sh! Quiet! Don't shoot, look at the sky!

KRAGLER: Go home too. All one has to do is what one wants. Because one mustn't do what the others want. And I want to go home. That's all I wanted. I ought to know. *Very calm.* I can't go on. *Silence.*

GLUBB: I don't know what to say to you. There's nothing in my mouth that would fit you.

KRAGLER: They poured your schnaps into the shit, brandy-seller, and they turned your farm into paper, Laar. But I've got my woman back.

After Glubb's 'So you've no sympathy for these people', etc. (p. 86) (his following remarks having been transposed as above) they move more or less straight on as in the 1922 edition to Carmen/Augusta's 'Then that was all lies, Africa and so on?' and to an extended version of Manke's 'The gentleman was bellowing like a stockbroker'. Right up to the attack on Anna by Laar and Manke (p. 51) the only substantial differences lie in Anna's silence and the absence of any clue as to how the fighting is going. This is given only when the shooting starts after Glubb has extricated Anna. The final section which follows is a good deal longer, but the changes are unimportant until everybody begins moving to the bridge. Then:

GLUBB: If he wants to go, let him. Don't stop him. Let him get into bed, we're fighting for him. Let them all do as they want, don't press them. He shouted for us, he went with us. There are so many of us, allow him to feel tired. We've got the room, we can accommodate lots of them. Admit him too, he still belongs to us.

KRAGLER *laughs raucously:* You people almost drowned at first with weeping at my story, and now you want to drag me down to the newspapers to get shot. Just because you've stuffed your heads with newspapers and novelettes, because you can't get grand opera out of your system. I barely managed to get my own wife; am I now supposed to liberate all yours? Free my neck so I can hang a hurdy-gurdy round it? And I simply washed my shirt in your tears. Ha ha ha ha! My flesh is to rot in the gutter so that your idea can come out on top! Are you drunk?

CARMEN: What nonsense is he talking? Come on! They've retreated. We'll still be in time for the attack!

BULLTROTTER: It's about time, damn you!

GLUBB *with simplicity and grandeur:* Tonight everybody must be out on the street. Tonight it will happen. Come with me, we must stick together now. Take each other by the hand and run for all you're worth. That's the way!

They run up the slope and vanish over the bridge. Glubb can still be heard, singing:

They'll have the whole damn lot –
Wife, land and all you've got.
Let them swallow it,
They'll get no benefit
The kingdom must be ours.

BABUSCH *flaps along after him:* There'll be heavy gunfire over Berlin in a quarter of an hour's time.

Exit across the bridge.

KRAGLER *piqued:* All right, go off to your newspaper buildings. Do yourselves in! If you won't let a man help you.

He throws dirt after them. Anna tries to come to him, but he thrusts her off and doesn't look her in the eyes.

ANNA: Andy! *She has sat down.* I must go home, Andy. I'm not going to have one. I'm not going to have a baby.

Kragler's long last speech, which follows, is basically the same as in the other two versions, including the anomalous mention of 'so early in the year'. Among the passages added are 'The shouting and that red moon they hoisted over the newspaper buildings: all of it's to swindle the people!', and

> Am I a baritone? Ha ha ha! Were you aiming to wash your dirty faces with tears once again? Did you want a swollen pregnant body floating down to the weir under the red moon? Was I myself to die in the newspaper buildings for you? Every evening? Did you want to have a good cry? Well, I'm going to bed. Would you like to help them? Rip the phrases from their throats! *Drumbeat.* Wash your own shirt! *Drumbeat.* Hang, hang yourselves if you don't get ahead!

Finally, in lieu of 'Very drunken and infantile' comes 'You can all stuff it. I'm the lover.'